TEILHARD EXPLAINED

TEILHARD
EXPLAINED

by
HENRI DE LUBAC, S.J.

translated by
ANTHONY BUONO

PAULIST PRESS DEUS BOOKS

NEW YORK   **GLEN ROCK**   **WESTMINSTER**

TORONTO   **AMSTERDAM**

A Deus Books Edition of Paulist Press, originally published under the title *Teilhard, Missionnaire et Apologiste* by Editions Priere et Vie, Toulouse, France, © 1966.

NIHIL OBSTAT:
Rev. John P. Haran, S.J.
Censor Deputatus

IMPRIMATUR:
✠ Bernard J. Flanagan, D.D.
Bishop of Worcester

January 11, 1968

Library of Congress
Catalog Card Number: 68-16677

Published by Paulist Press
Editorial Office: 304 W. 58th St., N.Y., N.Y. 10019
Business Office: Glen Rock, New Jersey 07452

Printed and bound in the
United States of America

CONTENTS

Contents

PART TWO

FROM THE WORLD TO GOD AND CHRIST IN THE WORK OF TEILHARD DE CHARDIN

APPENDICES AND NOTES

ACKNOWLEDGMENTS

THE APPEARANCE OF MAN by Pierre Teilhard de Chardin. Copyright 1956 by Editions du Seuil. Copyright © 1965 in the English translation by William Collins Sons & Co. Ltd., London, and Harper & Row, Publishers, Incorporated, New York.

THE DIVINE MILIEU by Pierre Teilhard de Chardin. Copyright 1957 by Editions de Seuil, Paris. English translation—Copyright © 1960 by Wm. Collins Sons & Co., London, and Harper & Row, Publishers, Incorporated, New York.

THE FUTURE OF MAN by Pierre Teilhard de Chardin, translated from the French by Norman Denny. Copyright 1959 by Editions du Seuil. Copyright © 1964 in the English translation by William Collins Sons & Co. Ltd., London, and Harper & Row, Publishers, Incorporated, New York.

HYMN OF THE UNIVERSE by Pierre Teilhard de Chardin (Harper & Row, 1965).

LETTERS FROM A TRAVELLER by Pierre Teilhard de Chardin. Copyright © 1962 in the English translation by William Collins & Co. Ltd., London, and Harper & Row, Publishers, Incorporated. Copyright © 1956, 1957 by Bernard Grasset.

THE MAKING OF A MIND by Pierre Teilhard de Chardin. Copyright © 1961 by Editions Bernard Grasset. Copyright © 1965 in the English translation by William Collins Sons & Co. Ltd., London, and Harper & Row, Publishers, Incorporated, New York.

MAN'S PLACE IN NATURE by Pierre Teilhard de Chardin. Copyright © 1956 by Editions Albin Michel. Copyright © 1966 in English translation by Williams Collins & Co. Ltd., London, and Harper & Row, Publishers, Incorporated.

THE PHENOMENON OF MAN by Pierre Teilhard de Chardin. Copyright 1955 by Editions du Seuil. Copyright © 1959 by Wm. Collins Sons & Co. Ltd., London, and Harper & Row, Publishers, Incorporated, New York. *Note:* Reprint only from 1965 Torchbook edition.

THE VISION OF THE PAST by Pierre Teilhard de Chardin. Copyright © 1966 in the English translation by William Collins & Co. Ltd., London, and Harper & Row, Publishers, Incorporated. Copyright © 1957 by Editions du Seuil.

FOREWORD

The two parts which comprise this slim volume reproduce and develop two conferences given at Rome in the autumn of 1965. The first took place at the *Domus Mariae* on October 15 under the auspices of the secretariat of the Brazilian episcopate; an abridged version appeared in the February 1966 issue of the periodical *Spiritus*. The second constituted a report presented to the sixth International Thomistic Congress in the grand ballroom of the Pallazzo of the *Cancellaria* at the request of Father Charles Boyer, S.J., secretary of the Academy of St. Thomas Aquinas and Thomistic Congresses. A résumé is scheduled to appear in the second volume of the *Proceedings* of the Congress.

We have avoided repeating herein what has already been set forth in our previous writings. However, the reader may complete the treatment of Teilhard the apologist by consulting the second part of our work *Teilhard de Chardin: The Man and His Meaning* (New York: The New American Library, 1967, A Mentor-Omega Book), pages 129–190, as well as several chapters of *The Religion of Teilhard de Chardin* (New York: Desclée Company, 1967).

The reader might also consult—particularly concerning the spiritual aspects of the subjects treated in this book—the *Correspondence* of Pierre Teilhard de Chardin and Maurice Blondel (New York: Herder and Herder, 1967).

TRANSLATOR'S NOTE

Before beginning the text proper of this remarkable work of Henri de Lubac a few preliminary remarks are in order. As he mentions in his Foreword, the author has written other books about his close friend Teilhard de Chardin which are much more lengthy and detailed than the present one.

Yet this deceptively slim volume with its seemingly restricted approach has captured the essence of both the thought and the person of Teilhard—the missionary and his apologetics. In so doing, Père de Lubac has earned the immense gratitude of all who have never had the time or the background to delve into Teilhard's works and ideas.

Furthermore, the noted author has done this in magnificent fashion. In a few broad strokes he gives us a glimpse of the trials and tribulations of the groping priest-scientist as well as the unswerving faith, unshakable hope, and indefatigable love of the dedicated man of God. He shows him grappling with the mysteries of the universe and the Christian Revelation, achieving a synthesis of the two and then humbly submitting all to the Church for approval.

At the same time Père de Lubac subtly and beautifully illustrates the words spoken by another world-renowned theologian, Karl Rahner, with reference to Teilhard: "Let us agree that even if Teilhard de Chardin has not in every respect succeeded in doing justice to dogma, then I would say *in magnis voluisse sat est*. That it isn't as bad as when we teachers of theology give forth with a very orthodox but sterile theology that is of interest to no one." [1]

It is crystal clear from the following pages that Teilhard is no "sterile repeater of [orthodox] statements" [2] but a seeker after truth no matter where found—and as such belongs to the spiritual lineage of St. Thomas Aquinas. At the same time it is equally—though completely unintentionally—demonstrated that Henri de Lubac is in the very same category.

The translation is in every way a completely faithful rendition of the original, except for the following variations and additions dictated by the nature of the book.

Whenever the author quotes from a work or letter of Teilhard that has already been translated into English, the existing English text is used and so indicated; otherwise a fresh translation is provided, based as much as possible on the style of the more prominent English editions of Teilhard's works. Since these have already set the example of avoiding the use of his frequent initial capitalizations, the present translation also eliminates the capitals which were naturally used in the French citations.

Again, for the convenience of the reader, the few French titles of works not yet translated which appear in the body of the work are immediately followed by an English equivalent in brackets. (Of course, wherever an English translation does exist it alone is mentioned.) This has not been done for the notes since it would have entailed too much repetition and confusion. Instead a complete list of all Teilhard's works mentioned in this book is appended at the end with the English equivalent alongside each (Appendix III).

For the further benefit of the reader a "Short Sketch of Teilhard's Life" (Appendix I) as well as a "Short Glossary of Teilhard's Vocabulary" (Appendix II) are also included. Finally, a rather complete *Index* has been added.

It goes without saying that these are all minor changes designed simply to aid in understanding the excellent substance of the text proper.

PART ONE

TEILHARD DE CHARDIN MISSIONARY AND DISCIPLE OF ST. PAUL

Introduction

In the words of Père René d'Ouince—one of his closest friends who knew him virtually "inside-out"—"Père Teilhard was of the blood of the great missionaries: a Nobili, a Ricci setting out for unknown continents, eager to win the earth for Jesus Christ." He cherished "the boundless, extravagant, ingenuous ambition to give the modern world" to Christ.[1]

On the day after his religious profession, while reflecting on a spiritual experience that was already lengthy and had been intense for some time, he had said to his Lord: "I belong to you. I must . . . propagate the Fire that you have communicated to me!"[2]

From that moment on the apostle, missionary, and propagator of the Fire to whom above all he was to recommend himself—and to whom he would always continue to do so—was St. Paul.

Teilhard's Favorite Saints

Père Teilhard de Chardin had a few favorite saints. First place was reserved for his patron St. Peter. For him, Peter was the symbol of the Faith both in his weaknesses and in his strength. In *La Foi qui opère* [*The Faith That Works*] (1918), he emphasized the Gospel account of Christ walking on the water:

Peter answered him and said, "Lord, if it is you, bid me come to you over the water." And he said, "Come." Then Peter got out of the boat and walked on the water to come to Jesus. But

seeing the wind was strong, he was afraid; and as he began to
sink he cried out, saying, "Lord, save me!" And Jesus at once
stretched forth his hand and took hold of him, saying to him,
"O you of little faith, why did you doubt?" [3]

He was forever meditating on this scene which recurs many
times in his works, correspondence, and retreat-notes over the
various stages of his life.[4] Peter the apostle was also, in his eyes,
the one whom the Lord must lead progressively along unforeseen
paths, "where [he] would not." [5] "To walk upon the waters
toward the Lord" and "to adore his hand upon us" represent
two essential and fundamental principles of the Teilhardian
spirituality.

Finally (we shall mention it quickly), just as the Apostle of
the Gentiles wishes to go up to Peter at Jerusalem and have his
"Gospel" approved in order not to risk "running in vain," in
like manner did Père Teilhard always conduct himself. We see
this in his repeated efforts to explain his sublime missionary
idea, in his never-ending journeyings to have the basis of his
spiritual teachings "approved" and "authenticated" in high
places, and lastly in his obedience, maintaining constant ties
with the responsible heads of the Church and keeping himself
in agreement with her spirit.

No more than Paul was he resigned to be solely a "spiritual
adventurer." [6] And his personal attitude was rooted in doctrinal
conviction: nothing in man's religious spirit has any value in the
final analysis, he reckoned, unless it converges on the "Roman
axis"; nothing is promised to life except that it must one day
flourish on the "Roman stock." [7]

Teilhard was also attracted to other saintly figures; for example, those two great founders of his own Order, Ignatius Loyola
and Francis Xavier, who can be likened in their respective mis-
sions to Peter and Paul. But Francis of Assisi also had a special
appeal for him. In Francis he admired on the one hand "the

vision of, and delight in, [God's] divinity present in all things" which transposed into another style were precisely his own, and on the other hand the prophetic mission of the saint who on the threshold of the 13th century renewed to some extent a Christianity that was languishing.[8]

Teilhard might well have written the words uttered by Paul VI on October 13, 1963: "Scientific progress, far from rendering religion vain, aids us to seek ever more sublime and profound comparisons. . . . It is to be hoped that this convergence heralds a new canticle of creatures, very different from the canticle of our brother Francis filled with beauty and candor, but . . . no less lyrical and mystical." [9] Can these words not be regarded as an ideal definition of the "lyrical and mystical" part of the Teilhardian work? Is not this new canticle of creatures a little of what has been termed—to designate the choice parts of this work—the "Hymn of the Universe"?

In St. Francis, different as he was from himself, Père Teilhard de Chardin recognized a model and precursor; better still, he recognized the precursor of the great missionary-to-come for whom he wished to prepare the way.[10]

Teilhard and St. Paul

Yet Teilhard's foremost teacher and inspirer was St. Paul. Like Saul of Tarsus, he was enraptured with "the incommunicable beauty of Christ." [11] Reared devoutly in a Christian family and ever faithful, Teilhard did not possess—like the persecutor-Pharisee—the shattering vision of Damascus; but he could say equally with him that he had seen Christ. More than once he had recourse to words such as "vision" and "seer" to depict his own experience.

As in the case of the Apostle, this vision was for Teilhard decisive. It constituted such an attraction for him that the words of Origen concerning Paul can be applied to him: "It is because of his extreme love for Jesus that he speaks of him without ceasing and, we might say, in a superfluous manner," [12] and he never ceased to revert to this love as to the ever-burning furnace of his interior life.[13]

To each of them, moreover, Jesus revealed himself *only* through an intimate relation to his "body." [14] Finally, for both the vision is fused with a call: it immediately engenders zeal for the conversion of the Gentiles. Pierre Teilhard declares with St. Paul: "Woe is me if I do not preach the Gospel!" Thus we see a rapid alternation during this period of intense spiritual activity from 1916 to 1920 between "mystical" writings and "apostolic" works—except when they blend into one as in *Le Prêtre* [*The Priest*].

However, after twenty centuries the world situation has changed. Who then are these Gentiles that Pierre Teilhard desires to uncover and encounter? What is this world for whose conversion he offers himself?

It has two principal traits. First of all, it is a considerably expanded world—a world henceforth complete, with the entire density of its past and all its spatial expanse. It is an earth now known to the very limits of its boundaries, explored in every sense, and unified in man's outlook. It embraces all civilizations, all religious forms, and the entire religious history of mankind— concerning which the first disciples of Jesus would have known only a few strictly local episodes—in the vast complexity of its ramifications.

All this represents rich food for reflection on the part of a Pierre Teilhard who learns to know it not only through books but through the circumstances of his itinerant life. It provides a multi-faceted attraction for his apostolic soul. Many times, from China, he directs an urgent invitation to his friends. Here, he tells them, throughout the Far East we are waiting for a work which will set forth the Essence of Christianity or the Christian viewpoint in contrast to Confucianism, or Buddhism, or Hinduism. It must be something both profound and concrete, something simple and vibrant—an exposition with depth and serenity, skillfully emphasizing the essential. Who then will give us this new *Summa ad Gentiles,* he asks in his dream.[15]

His first candidate for such a task was Pierre Charles, professor of dogma at Louvain who had been the companion of his theological studies at Hastings.[16] He was the most suitable of all. But almost immediately Teilhard despaired of tieing down his friend's exuberant activity for the length of time required. Accordingly, he addressed himself to others, well aware that his own specialization did not allow him to see the project through to the end.[17]

Nevertheless, after a multiplicity of contacts, he did tackle the task himself in a series of brief writings which represent an outline of, or a prolegomena to, his thought. He concentrates on showing "the place of Christianity in the world," [18] or setting forth the major lines of "the Christian vision of the universe"; he sketches the tableau of a "Mystique of the West" inspired by Christian personalism, in contrast to the pantheisms of India and the other doctrines of identity, etc.

But at the same time he establishes with greater emphasis that in its most dynamic part, which ever remains the West, ours is a new world. It is a world formed by the new disciplines of the positive sciences; a world of technology whereby men are refashioned, so to speak; a world of research, bearer of new ideas and new hopes; a world of evolution which forces us to readjust our mental categories.

This is the world—whose birth he realized before most of his contemporaries—to which Pierre Teilhard is attached by one whole part of himself. And it is in relation to this world that he has his proper mission. He hears its secret call, as Paul heard the call of Macedonia—and Greece and Rome and Spain; and as Francis Xavier heard the call of India and Japan and China.

"There," he exclaims, "lie the Indies that call me more strongly than St. Francis Xavier's!" [19]

However, he quickly adds: "But what a vast problem to be solved, no longer of ritual but of ideas, before one can really convert them!" For in effect, "because of one reason or another —and for the first time since the Christian era began—a human civilization has been established lacking the explicit consciousness of Christ." [20] "Pagans in the traditional sense of the term were or are 'residuals.' But we are at present faced with an emerging human current. This is a novel situation and demands a new method of attack and conversion." [21]

In this present humanity, the revelation acquired from its own history and the astonishingly varied riches of its own creations has given evidence of the germ of a radical relativism; the conviction that the new forces obtained through technology enables it to dominate nature has suggested to it with a kind of headiness the idea of its own self-sufficiency;[22] finally, by an inverse phenomenon of appearance in the face of a world suddenly grown to infinite dimensions the traditional concepts of divinity have paled in its eyes; in short, "humanity has momentarily lost its God." [23]

Furthermore, during this time—despite a considerable missionary effort—Christianity seems to have slowly retrogressed in the idea it has of itself and the way in which it is lived by the mass of its adherents or by a certain number of its theoreticians; it has turned inward toward itself, in a reflex of frightened defense; the life-sap of the Spirit circulates only in a diminishing manner in this vast body. In short, concludes Teilhard, "we have *ceased* to be contagious."

There in one sobering word is indicated the great difference between the situation of the first Christian generations—who might appear to be threatened with extinction in the bosom of a hostile world—and the situation he observed in our time. This is not to say that our faith no longer has in itself the same power of truth and salvation; rather, he explains, "we no longer have a *vital* conception of the world to be produced. It is a situation that strikes our eyes as soon as we step out of the churches and seminaries." [24]

But believer that he is, Pierre Teilhard is not disheartened by this. The gravity of the situation, to which he periodically calls the attention of his superiors, only increases his missionary fervor at the same time that it determines its orientation.

"My Gospel and my mission is to bring Christ by virtue of properly organic attachments, to the very heart of realities reputed to be the most dangerous, naturalistic, and pagan." [25] This is how he expressed himself in a context of prayer on the day after his religious profession; he was to resume the thought the following year in a work intended especially for a few theologians and religious leaders—one of the boldest works ever to issue from his pen containing at times the least defensible of formulas: [26] "It is good to extend the kingdom of God to new peoples. It is even better and more direct to *cause it to penetrate* to the profound 'nisus' in which all of humanity's desires are presently reunited." [27]

Then speaking from the viewpoint of the world, he strives to discern therein the still undiscovered element which must ready it for conversion: "I am sure that the society around us contains a point that is vulnerable to the penetration of the Spirit of God. I am convinced that there is massed about us an enormous religious potential which however does not succeed in being tapped." [28]

Then returning to the viewpoint of Christianity, he repeats that "if Christ is risen," his power of renewal and transformation is intact forever. He thus establishes the "insufficiency of an *excessively* 'detached' Christianity," as well as "an exclusively lay worship of the earth, to nourish the whole human heart and to subsist in isolation"; he will therefore dispense all his strength to effect that "meeting the truth which is unfolded on earth, the Truth descended from heaven will synthesize all the world's hopes in the blessed Reality of Christ, whose Body is the Center of the Chosen Life." [29]

In Search of New Gentiles

"The blessed Reality of Christ!" It is here that Pierre Teilhard de Chardin places himself more especially in the line of St. Paul.[30]

He reads and continually rereads the Pauline Epistles. He fashions a little notebook for himself that will be his companion for many years in which he copies the Christological texts of the Apostle together with those of St. John. He has pored over them in a favorable climate during the course of his theological studies; he continues to meditate on them, wishing to understand them "without attenuation and without gloss." [31] Père Emile Rideau has drawn up a list of the texts which he utilizes in his written work:[32] though the citations are frequent, the number of texts cited is not large: some twelve or fifteen; but they are very typical, and they are not brought into his developments simply as decorative or confirmatory material. They constitute inspirational texts.

Père Teilhard does not usually go into details of philology or history, or any critical discussion regarding them—he did not profess to be an exegete; but he has pondered their essential meaning and he asks how they should be received by us today as Christians of the 20th century so as to retain their full meaning in our minds.

Thus, with the Epistles as a starting point, he will elaborate his teaching on "the cosmic Christ," or "the universal Christ," which later becomes the doctrine of "the evolutive Christ." For this, he undertakes to Christianize the new dynamic representation of the cosmos—just as Paul had to Christianize certain Stoic views.

There must be in the cosmos, he believes, "a privileged place where as in some universal boulevard everything is seen, everything is felt, everything is commanded, everything is animated, and everything is touched. Is this not a wondrous spot in which to place—or better acknowledge—Jesus? . . . He is the First and he is the Head. In him all things have been created, and all things hold together, and all things are consummated." Thus we see him rejoice and be distended in these perspectives. Not for an instant does he doubt that they are not "in striking harmony with the fundamental texts" of St. Paul as well as St. John and the Greek Fathers.[33]

Evidently, we can ask if the work of continuation and transposition, which Père Teilhard realizes in this way, succeeds in finding its perfect expression.[34] We can also debate the question of knowing whether, for example, in his use of a word like "pleroma" he is fully in accord with his model. The answer in this case will depend on the conclusions of the exegetes, who are not agreed among themselves. Indeed, the Teilhardian use of the word is found to be authorized by the exegesis of Pierre Benoît.[35] However, this is a secondary question.

What is more important and indeed of paramount interest is the question of knowing whether the Teilhardian ideas of the cosmic Christ and the universal Christ do or do not reproduce the principal components of the Pauline idea. We believe we can give an affirmative answer to this question.

First of all, no matter what has been said, St. Paul teaches a true action not only of the Word but of Christ—and more especially of the risen Christ—over the cosmos, and this dominating action is essentially a unifying one. It began to be exercised the moment the world came into existence. This tells us immediately the texts which Père Teilhard loves to cite: *In ipso condita sunt universa. . . . Omnia in ipso constant,* etc. [In him all things were made. . . . In him all things hold together.][36]

Those who regard the idea of a cosmic activity of Christ as

"unacceptable" either have not studied the texts of the Apostle closely, or make too little of them; neither have they to any greater extent envisaged "the cosmological role of Wisdom," whose attributes are applied to Christ by the New Testament.[37]

Further, no more for Père Teilhard de Chardin than for St. Paul is this cosmic Christ—in whatever way one might wish to understand him later—a kind of organism that would have only a more or less extrinsic relationship with the personal being whose name history knows as Jesus of Nazareth. For him as for Paul, the Person of Jesus Christ is in the words of Charles-Harold Dodd author of the work *The Meaning of Paul for Today"* intensely individual and yet wonderfully universal." [38]

It is really Jesus himself who is at the head of the whole Body and its unifying principle, and his organic influence extends throughout the universe. It is the same Word of God who was made man in the womb of the Virgin, died on Calvary, and rose on the third day. *Descendit, et ascendit, ut impleret omnia* [He descended and ascended, that he might fill all things].

Once again it is a text of St. Paul that his disciple loves to cite and summarize; it is even through this same text—he once confided to Père Pierre Leroy—that he most freely expressed all his religious thought, all his mystique. This enables us to understand his special devotion to the mystery of the ascension whose feast he annually celebrated with love.

By this same fact, finally, it is clear that the growth of the cosmic Christ and his fulfillment-to-come do not at all affect or in any way compromise the eternal actuality of the divine Word or the initial historical reality of the incarnate Word:[39] "The immense enchantment of the divine *milieu* owes all its value in the long run to the human-divine contact which was revealed at the Epiphany of Jesus. . . . The mystical Christ, the universal Christ of St. Paul, has neither meaning nor value in our eyes except as an expansion of the Christ who was born of Mary and who died on the cross." [40] "If our Lord Jesus Christ does not have a personal and objective reality, the entire Christian religious current vanishes—and the world is left without an Omega point.

"But we must explore the cosmic profundity of Christ." [41]

The Cosmic Christ

In what then does the newness consist with respect to St. Paul? In this, as we have said, that in a universe conceived of as evolving (in the complete sense of the word, no longer only tellurical or biological, but spiritual [42]), the cosmic Christ must be called the "evolutive Christ." For, if everything has been created in Christ "as in the supreme center of harmony and cohesion which gives the world its meaning, its value, and thereby its reality," to use the words of Père Joseph Huby in his commentary on the Epistle to the Ephesians;[43] and if, in the words of Père Teilhard, "the universal Christ means that Christ exerts a physical influence on all things"; then to maintain this total influence he must be conceived of as exerting himself in some manner over the evolution of the world.

On this precise point, Père Teilhard again follows St. Paul. He is more seriously faithful to St. Paul, at least in principle, than if he were merely content to repeat his formulas. The Apostle, as we have seen above, incorporated into his conception of Christ a certain number of Stoic views that had become current in his day:[44] Teilhard intends to continue Paul's process, by incorporating into the same basic Christian conception the evolutionary views characteristic of our age. Similarly, just as Paul completely transformed those views, purifying them of their original pantheism, so does Teilhard continue to do today.

With some measure of astonishment, Teilhard ascertained that "the theory of the universal Christ as taught by St. Paul"—a theory in which he saw "the very marrow of the Christian tree swollen with sap"—has yielded only little fruit until our day. Accordingly, he believed that the time is now ripe "to resume its growth." Yet in thus seeking to achieve "the synthesis of the new and the old," he regards himself in no way as an "innovator." He refuses this designation.

In his view, no modification touches upon the articles of faith as such. These (to which we will return) remain unchanged in their substance, even if they must be explained by new applications and become the principle of new syntheses. "Applied to the new turn taken by the human spirit, the moral and intellectual directives contained in Revelation are preserved without change in relationships that give the essential figure of Christ and of the Christian." [45] It is always a question of preserving and proclaiming "the essential function as consummator assumed by the risen Christ as the center and peak of creation." [46]

The observation has been justly made that "neither the Gospel, nor St. John, nor St. Paul, has experienced or had any need to experience this evolutionary vision" [47] which is unfolded in the Teilhardian work. The observation is evident and in addition imposes itself on every Christian. Père Teilhard readily subscribed to it. Even more, he advanced it. "Through the Incarnation," he wrote, "God descends into nature to super-animate it and lead it back to him"; in itself, he believed, this dogma can be adapted to a good many diverse representations of the experimental world, and he ascertained that in fact Christians never incurred difficulty in considering their faith within the framework of a static universe.[48]

However, it does not follow that to preserve in our day both the fullness and the urgency of the affirmations of a St. Paul or a St. John we do not perhaps have to transpose "in terms of cosmogenesis the traditional vision expressed in terms of cosmos," [49] and consequently to translate the idea of a mastery of Christ over the cosmos in terms of the corresponding idea of "an evolutive Christ." [50]

Such at least was Père Teilhard's conviction, and we do not see that there is anything unacceptable about it *a priori*—rather, the contrary is evident. Doubtless, such a transposition, entailing such a translation, will pose more than one problem in which the faith may find itself involved and which it does not pertain to any one man to resolve—or even to perceive in a completely distinct manner. Thus, in his view which has remained that of a man of science, Père Teilhard did not analyze nor even completely envisage the kind of distinction and the type of relation that exists between the natural history of the world, human history, and the history of salvation; these would have led him to make a good many complementary precisions concerning the role of Christ.

These are inadequacies that might be termed inevitable; nor did they entirely escape Teilhard's attention, although he did not perceive them with complete clarity. It suffices that in undertaking "to disengage dogmatically in the person of Christ the cosmic face and function which constitute him organically as the prime mover and director, the 'soul' of evolution," he remained within the logic of the Pauline thought.

This is the point that Père Joseph Maréchal had perceived at Louvain. He once wrote to Père Teilhard, after reading one of his essays *Christologie et Evolution* [*Christology and Evolution*]: "Like yourself I believe that the 'well understood' progress of natural philosophy should enrich our understanding of the mystery of the Incarnation and give a more real content to the very beautiful expressions of St. John and St. Paul which we have preserved without sufficiently 'realizing' their primary significance." [51]

Père Teilhard had himself posed the problem very well: "What must Christology become *if it is to remain itself?*" [52] A bit later, he similarly defined its purpose, specifying that for him it was a question of nothing else but to "preserve for Christ the same qualities which form the basis for his power and our adoration." [53]

Dogma does not keep itself alive in the integrity of its substance unless it retains its assimilative force in the mind of the believer. Newman wrote in a page of his *Development,* a book which Père Teilhard read very carefully and which provoked lengthy reflections on his part: "Was [the Christianity lived by the Fathers of the Church] unitive? Had it the power, while keeping its own identity, of absorbing its antagonists, as Aaron's rod, according to St. Jerome's illustration, devoured the rods of the sorcerers of Egypt? Did it incorporate them into itself, or was it dissolved into them?" [54]

This interrogation does not concern only primitive Christianity; it remains actual from age to age. We fully realize that the work of Père Teilhard de Chardin presents it with a new occasion to arise. But we must be persuaded of it: if there is always a danger in ourselves that the Christian faith might experience death by dissolution, there is also—something certain conservative spirits are too prone to forget and in forgetting it they thereby increase the first danger for others—another symmetrical danger, the danger of death by estrangement and separation. When truth is no longer fruitful, it is close to death. If the danger on either side were avoided, it would not be difficult to see on which side can be found the spirit of St. Paul, that is, the true missionary spirit, essential to the Christian spirit.

This has been perfectly grasped by Jacques-Albert Cuttat, who could not fail to encounter the work of Père Teilhard when he undertook to examine whether the Christian experience is capable of assuming Oriental spirituality:

Examined, weighed, and judged in the light of a theology whose Object is Someone and not Something, . . . the basic inspiration of Père Teilhard de Chardin's work—so revolutionary on the surface—reveals its profound biblical and traditional core. Have the defenders of an immobile ecclesial traditionalism, a static fidelity to the Catholic splendors of the past, given thought to the frightful "backlash shock" that threatens a Christian conscience *pretending to ignore* the fact that "we are today assisting at a changing face of nature which holds prodigies?"

Do they sufficiently realize that we need *more*—not *less*—faith in the Word through whom "all things were made . . . , and without [whom] was made nothing that has been made" (Jn. 1, 3) and in the "Father [who] works" without ceasing (Jn. 5, 17), in order to safeguard and preserve intact in the midst of the 20th century—"to conserve" while revitalizing—the conviction that "the better we know nature, the better we will be able to know God" (Etienne Gilson)?

Is there a more Catholic and more Orthodox task than the renewal of the Christocentric cosmology of St. Paul and the Greek Fathers undertaken on the level of our astronomical, geological, biological, and anthropological horizon which has become so vast since then as to appear to so many cultured minds—believers included—as incapable of being set against a personal transcendence? [55]

Concern for the Church

Shifting our gaze from the teaching to the man, we see that several characteristics of his missionary spirit cannot fail to remind us again of the Apostle to the Gentiles.

Both men appear borne up by a great spirit of Christian freedom: that freedom which is in no way tinged with anarchy, and which arises not from one's own person but from the Spirit of God. It is a freedom which disposes one for magnificent new tasks, which leads to them even before being able to distinguish the concrete conditions, and which thus requires abandonment of self.

We already discern such a freedom in the reflections which Pierre Teilhard disclosed to his friend Auguste Valensin, from

1920 on, as when he began to foresee the difficulties he would encounter in his teaching and in his Parisian apostolate:

> The worst thing that could befall me is to be sent off to one of those distant shores which I ask only to go find and work in. It is a great release no longer to prize anything but the truth, and to be convinced that sooner or later Our Lord will bring together in synthesis within himself the whole of this truth and all our clumsy or feeble efforts to attain it.[56]

But once difficulties arise, when he encounters an obstacle of whatever kind which might seem to stand in the way of the Gospel's penetration without any apparent remedy, the soul of the missionary is filled with another type of sentiment. Thus a cry is torn from this soul captivated by Christ and seeking only his kingdom: *"Cupio dissolvi et esse cum Christo"* ["I wish to be dissolved and to be with Christ"].

Certainly, in Père Teilhard's case the obstacle took other forms than those described for us by the Pauline Epistles. It arose partly from his own imprudences and from the still overly imperfect expression given here or there to his message. Yet, even in this respect, a profound similarity is undeniable. The pain of the missionary—which brings him to the edge of discouragement and wrings his cry out of him—reaches him from the obstacle encountered not without but within the Church.

In the case of St. Paul, this obstacle was primarily the opposition of the Judaizing circles; for Pierre Teilhard it will be what he calls "this frightful inertia" of a more or less official theology which will give him the impression—the illusion?—that there is no longer any escape for him except in death:

> I am interiorly gripped by two divergent forces: the first consists in the ever more "harsh" view that there is no other escape from life than Our Lord, and the second consists in the even more accentuated sentiment, perhaps, of what is gross, narrow, and fallible in the present Church. This leads me at times to

think: "Cupio dissolvi" ["I desire to be dissolved"] in order to escape this bond.[57]

If we cannot in toto adopt his point of view which often allowed him to see only one aspect of things, we can at least retain—from this analysis of such firm characteristics—the subjective analogy with the sentiment of St. Paul. But the analogy becomes once again completely objective when we observe on one side and the other the same concern for the Church.

We have already mentioned the need experienced by both men to be recognized by Peter in order to be assured of not having "run in vain." Such a preoccupation constantly haunted Père Teilhard. Already instructed by an initial saddening experience,[58] which afforded him a glimpse of the future under rather somber colors, he nevertheless wrote on December 31, 1926:

It is possible that it may be my destiny to live until the end marginally to official ideas and attitudes; but on my side I would do anything to put an end to that situation.

Two months later he wrote to his friend Abbé Gaudefroy, professor at the "Institut Catholique" of Paris: "I wish I could dispel . . . the cloud that hangs between Rome and myself." [59] This caused him to conceive a bold project which was to be realized only more than twenty years later:

Do you think it impossible that I might one day go to Rome (without a rope around my neck) and try to explain to those in authority the kind of evangelization I feel called to and the methods I seek in order to understand (possibly, too well), and to speak, the language of people who are as far removed from us as (and even more interesting than) the Chinese?

On another occasion he declared: "I would very much like

to try something at Rome—to make them see what I see." And the fact is that he did try—on many occasions and in various ways. Letters, submission of manuscripts, conversations with his superiors, memoirs set down especially for them—all while awaiting the lengthy Roman visit of autumn 1948, which was itself followed by other manuscripts submitted and further correspondence!

He never became discouraged: on Good Friday of 1955, two days before his death, he addressed another confidential letter to his Provincial setting forth some of his most cherished ideas.[60] He would no longer waver in the conviction that the Church—the visible Church which wields power over us at times in grueling fashion—is "the Body of Christ and never to be abandoned"; for she alone "guarantees my objective contact with the Other," and she alone "holds the future stability of the cosmos":

Indeed, the more I strive, in love and wonder, to measure the huge movements of past life in the light of paleontology, the more I become convinced that this majestic process, *which nothing can arrest,* can achieve its consummation only in becoming Christianized.[61]

Never did he doubt "the position of Catholicism as the central axis in the convergent bundle of human activities." [62] On December 13, 1918 he had written: "For me, the Church is the (axial) current of life; it seems to me that this conviction is capable of resisting all doubts and every scandal," and again in 1950 in an anticipatory view he will speak of the confluence to be effected "on the Christian axis, between the stream channeled by ancient mystiques and the more recent but rapidly increasing flood of the sense of evolution." [63] In his particular language he knew how to express his confidence in the unique and irreplaceable role which the Church of Christ has received from her founder:

At the very heart of the social phenomenon, a kind of *ultra-socialization* is in progress: that whereby the "Church" is being formed little by little, vivifying by its influence and collecting under their sublimest form all the [spiritual] energies of the noosphere; the Church, reflectively "Christified" portion of the world; the Church, main focus of inter-human affinities via super-charity; the Church, central axis of universal convergence and exact point of encounter flashing between universe and the Omega point.[64]

Whatever rightly or wrongly seemed to him subject to criticism in the Church of his time, that "frightful rubbish" with which he sometimes saw her encumbered—a missionary of the following generation would call it: "her excess baggage" [65]—did not prevent him from believing and hoping. Neither did what he ascertained from the scientific viewpoint concerning "her incredible present inadequacy." Nor for that matter did what he had to suffer personally at the hands of a few persons in the Church.

It is understood of course that none of this ever took place without a struggle; but he believed in the triumph of the "impossible" both in the spiritual world as well as in the biosphere. Refusing to dwell on criticisms, he was happy to perceive signs of a growing vigor in the life of the Church:

So many contacts with men of all ages have filled me with hope. I am more and more convinced that something grand is presently being born in the bosom of the Church—something that will convert the earth in a contagious manner. . . .

It was in 1936 that he set down these lines, thus replying to his statement of a little earlier, the mark of an apparently disabused realism, which we have cited above: "We have ceased to be contagious." Thanks to this "something," this "something grand" whose birth he foresaw, he could still say in 1948—after again affirming the inadequacies of the time: "I am convinced that the Christian Faith will make the world resound anew."

A New Nicaea

Located as she is within the heart of a humanity which is "in the process of melting," "there is no reason for us to be astonished that the Church is also going through a "melting" period, making a "reform necessary." This reform, adds Père Teilhard in a letter of 1950 whose upshot we will shortly see, will not be "a simple affair of institutions and *mores* but of *Faith*." This can be understood in various senses.

Did Père Teilhard take this to mean that the traditional Faith of the Church must be substantially changed? Not at all. To interpret it in such fashion would be grossly to misunderstand his thought. And it would be necessary to make light of his own explanations.

On the contrary, he believes that the Faith of the Church in connection with man's newly acquired sense of the future must grow in some way by developing the potentialities contained in the living treasure of Revelation. This will be, he concludes, a rejuvenated Christianity, "not through the alteration of its structure but through the assimilation of new elements"; it will be "the Christianity faithfully prolonged unto the limits of itself." [67]

The whole Teilhardian program in this regard is summed up in a "new Christology"; this is again a word that speaks of change, but he tells us that it must be understood simply as a Christology "extended to the organic dimensions of our new universe." He goes on to explain further that it is a question of endowing the traditional Christology with an increase of actuality and vitality";[68] of demonstrating to everyone in the face of the "almost limitless extensions" of the world that "our Christ" is "capable of spanning and illuminating them." And it is once again a text of St. Paul that Teilhard cites on this subject: *"Neque longitudo, neque latitudo, neque profundum"* ["Neither length, nor height, nor depth"].[69]

Nothing will ever replace "our Christ." "Never has he been

found lacking." [70] Consequently, not only is there no idea of some other Christ—this is more than evident—but neither is there any idea of replacing the inherited and established Christology with some other Christology. He intends (and he will one day write this to Rome) to proceed, through the entire progression of his thought, in the opposite direction of modernism, "a movement which diminished the reality and grandeur of Christ."

What he calls for wholeheartedly is not an abandonment or any diminution of the Faith of Nicaea; it is as he tells us "a new Nicaea" which will complete the first. Just as the first Nicaea (subsequently completed) defined Christ's relationship to God, so will this new Nicaea define his relationship to the universe, finally giving their full weight to St. Paul's statements that are at the same time Christic and cosmic. [71] For "we may say that the dominant concern of theologians in the first centuries of the Church was to determine the position of Christ in relation to the Trinity. In our time the vital question has become the following: to analyze and specify exactly, in its relations, the existence of the influence that holds together Christ and the universe." [72]

This idea pursued Teilhard. On several occasions, he spoke about it to his friends and wrote about it to his superiors. As early as 1918 in the first redaction of *Mon Univers* [*My Universe*] he had expressed this desire: "I hope . . . —with every desire I have to love God—that the elements of truth which are universally believed and professed by the Church concerning the action and universal presence of God and Christ may finally be considered *as a whole and without attenuation*." [73] Less than two months before his death he was to express it anew: "We have need of a new Nicaea." [74]

Six years later to everyone's amazement, John XXIII convoked a Council. It was not exactly a case of a new Nicaea, but of a new Vatican. The agenda did not concern precisely the relations of Christ to the universe but those of the Church to the modern world. However, it was already the breath of renewal for which he had waited, hoped, and prayed; and whose advance signs he had heralded with joy.[75] Furthermore, in the context of the Council when one wished to pursue reflection to the very ultimate foundation of proclaimed doctrine concerning the relations of the Church to the world, it was really on the relation of the universe to Christ that attention had to be focused.

Listen to Père Teilhard describing for us the first phases of the operation from which he told his readers "the Religion of tomorrow is making ready to arise"—in a vocabulary whose apologetic intent must not be overlooked:

> It seems evident that directed by a divine instinct, and in parallel fashion to the rise of modern human aspirations, the Christian sap is already beginning to flow so as to flower in the shoot so long dormant. Begun two centuries ago by the cult of the Heart of Jesus, a profound movement is clearly visible in the Church toward the adoration of Christ considered in his influences over the mystical Body and consequently over the entire social organism. . . . Lastly, by an action that expresses a decisive stage in the formulation of dogma, Rome has transferred and consecrated into the figure of Christ the King this forward and irresistible march of the Christian consciousness toward a more universalist and realistic appreciation of the Incarnation.
>
> My idea and my dream would be that, by a logical prolongation of the same movement, the Church should explicitate and present to the world—as St. Paul had already done for his converts—the magnificent figure of him in whom the Pleroma finds its physical beginning, its expression and stability: the Omega Christ, the universal Christ.[76]

The difference or rather the prolongation, the deepening, the added step taken forward under the guidance of St. Paul, in going from Christ the King to the universal Christ so as to demonstrate more clearly that Christ "is not a king in our sense of the term" [77] would be the passage from a still excessively unilateral juridic representation to a more organic one. Such was his thought and such did he express it in 1940 at Peking in a brief memoir which he entitled "La Parole attendue" [The Long-Awaited Word].

This dream had in his eyes nothing unreal about it: "For is it not part of the customary economy of the Christian life that in the data of Revelation certain elements for a long time dormant should suddenly develop into living branches upon the demand and in the measure of new times and new needs?" *Nova et Vetera* [New and Old].

On December 13, 1952 he was to write from New York to his old friend Abbé Henri Breuil: "If I were to become pope, what a time to write an encyclical on the universal Christ!" Beneath the form of a pleasant proposal, lay ever the same desire, the same dream, and the same hope.

The Long-Awaited Transformation

Casting a roundabout eye on the different religions and diverse spiritual movements on this planet, he concluded: "Only Christianity remains standing, capable of measuring up to the intellectual and moral world that has arisen in the West after the Renaissance." [78] Then, fixing his attention on her, he concluded: "The Church is as living as ever; you have only to allow her to grow." [79]

Hence, when one day he had to reply to a priest who had left the Catholic Church and seemed to be inviting him to do likewise upon learning that Teilhard believed in a necessary and even—as we have seen—a kind of "melting" reform, he could still say:

I see ever more that there is no better way for me to promote what I anticipate than to work for reform (as defined above) *from within:* that is, in sincere attachment to the "phylum" whose development I await.[80] Very sincerely (and without wishing to criticize your action!), only in the Roman stock taken in its integral unity can I see biological support sufficiently wide and sufficiently variegated to operate and maintain the transformation we await. Neither is this pure speculation. For half a century I have seen at too close range the revitalization of Christian life and thought—in spite of any encyclical [81]—not to have immense confidence in the re-animating powers of the ancient Roman stock.[82]

By an astonishing example of rank prejudice a critic has preferred to see in this page—wherein Père Teilhard proclaims his "immense confidence" and wherein everything exudes the most complete and delicate sincerity—only an abyss of duplicity, and has chosen to infer the admission of a kind of plot against the Church! [83] In contradiction to all that we know of Teilhard as well as against this text itself, he shows Teilhard succumbing in darkness to the establishment of a new faith which would in his opinion supplant the Christian faith!

This critic argues for the application to Teilhard of the most severe passage of the encyclical *Pascendi,* castigating the hypocrisy of those who "concealing an unlimited rashness beneath lies of submission," would hide themselves within the Church with the purpose of more surely bringing about her ruin. And he would have us recognize Teilhard as bearing a "crying resemblance" to these "worst enemies of the Church." How true it is that everything can be given a perverse meaning!

Yet, not one word in this letter would lead us to think that the labor of reform to be accomplished "from within" must entail any kind of abandonment or be carried out in the secret of "a member of the underground." Everything in it shows— in conformity with other texts we have cited as well as the constant behavior of the religious toward his superiors—that it is from the Church herself, the ancient Roman stock, that the author again expects that miracle of renewal which is produced within her bosom from age to age.[84] And he does so because he has been confirmed in his faith by the experience of a lifetime—an experience that has nothing esoteric about it.

To escape this evidence our critic is obliged to misrepresent the letter cited, as we have just said, and furthermore to suppose that Teilhard spent his life in deceiving his brothers in religion and his best friends, the very persons before whom he was accustomed to lay bare his bouts of conscience.

Teilhard's correspondent, however, was not deceived. Commenting on these lines which he received, truly written from one priest to another, he declared: Teilhard "has always believed that the necessary transformations would be undertaken and resolved by the very initiative of his Church." [85] In fact, in order to reveal his sinister program to him, this strange conspirator had sent the former priest a copy of the memoir submitted two years previously to the Roman authorities—and a few of the very texts regarded by some as the most rash of all had already appeared in an even earlier memoir also written at the request of the counselors given him by God.

In this same autumn of 1950, Teilhard addressed another confidential Note to his superiors at Rome (nor was this to be the last) with the sole purpose of providing a detailed treatment of one of the subjects which might have appeared to disquiet them the most. He thus acted—as he had long before resolved to do—"without any compromise or artifice." This represented on his part a gesture of trust and courageous loyalty, so much the more meritorious as his personal situation ran the risk of becoming more aggravated by it; furthermore, we should emphasize that such a gesture was entirely incompatible with the attitude which we have noted was imputed to him and, all to the contrary, in perfect conformity with what the Church expects from her children.[86]

In short, if we were to seek a term of comparison to explain the personal attitude which Père Teilhard de Chardin described to his correspondent, it is not in some crypto-modernist that we will chance to find it; rather it is in the author of a very recent work of great significance who tells us: "We cannot reform a body, no matter how small, by threat of division. It is always from within and with an infinite patience that we can revitalize what it should be." [87] (These are the words of Brother Roger Schutz, prior of Taizé.)

Missionary Faith

In virtue of the inspiration that motivated his entire work and his whole behavior, Père Teilhard de Chardin was a true missionary. "The experience of a life spent simultaneously at the core of the Gentiles and at the core of the Church" [88] give his thought taken as a whole a depth lacking to so many others. This may at times have given "the impression of temerity or irreverence," and as such represents another trait of similarity to the great Apostle whose freedom with words did not fail to offend several of his contemporaries, while waiting to be the subject of abuse on the part of others over the course of the centuries.

But basically this was nothing more (in his case as in St. Paul's) than "an intrepid confidence in the victory of Jesus Christ," [89] just as there was nothing more at the bottom of the daring aspects of his program than the desire "that his Face might be revealed more and more."

An author who evinces no sympathy for the Teilhardian synthesis has nevertheless acknowledged the purity of his inspiration in a beautifully expressed testimony which is especially worth repeating. Etienne Gilson has written:

All of St. Paul stands out in Teilhard in passing through him, because the Teilhardian element harbors the nugget of pure gold which has the piety and faith of his youth—it lies intact, as if it has been miraculously preserved beneath the continual deposits of scientific or philosophical material. He himself stressed this continuity, an element essential to the understanding of his writings. The cosmic Christ was for him first of all the Child Jesus, and he must always remain so. The newborn of Christmas is precisely the same one who becomes the child of Bethlehem and the Crucified, the Mover and the fundamental Core of the world itself.

His readers can indeed receive from Teilhard the letter of his cosmic views, the notions and concepts conveying his thought; but they cannot receive from him his own religious experience, that faith so simple, so pure and so total that nothing ever weakened it and which is essential to the meaning of his work. One cannot be a mediocre Christian and believe himself capable of living the thought of Père Teilhard de Chardin.[90]

Père Teilhard's vocation was too individual for us to be able to set it up as a norm. The Christian and the priest have other concrete ways—more normal or at least more ordinary—in which to follow Christ and imitate St. Paul. Besides Père Teilhard never pretended to formulate a complete theology in his thoughtful work. Most often, he is unilateral in searching for it or in its discovery. Finally, in what he believed to have found of the truth, he did not succeed in saying everything; and even what he did say, he quite possibly did not always say too well.

Teilhard himself often noted this twofold limitation in terms whose absolute sincerity can be guaranteed by those who knew him well. He often acknowledged "the approximate and inadequate aspects of [his] attempts at explanation"; he desired readers capable of making an effort to perceive the basic orientations at times veiled "beneath inadequate expressions."

"I am feeling my way," he once wrote to a theologian who had consulted him, "just as you are. All I shall ever be able to do is to give you a number of suggestions. But, surely, it is upon this hesitant, shared work of those who believe that God sends down the truly creative action of his light." Hence, more

than once he modestly appealed to others to translate his own
thought, when it might seem necessary, into a more traditional
language.[91] This merely acknowledges something he himself
realized, that he is not an accomplished master nor always a
very certain one. It has even been written with good reason that
he "did not consider himself a master and did not seek to recruit
disciples." [92]

Nevertheless, in his missionary fervor which placed him in a
certain measure so close to St. Paul, he can serve as our model.
Even today, in a situation already quite different from the one
he knew until his last years, he can help us by his tried and
tested faith to surmount a spiritual crisis whose effects will
have repercussions even on certain theories concerning the
mission of the Church.

On the fringe, completely on the fringe of the conciliar *aggi-
ornamento* (which would have made him so happy), certain
generalities about "the overture to the world," about "the service
of the world" (the expression is Père Teilhard's) or about
"implicit Christianity," about "the anonymous Christians," about
"the spirit of dialogue," about "the comprehension of atheism"
are sometimes stripped of the excellent meaning they can—
and indeed often do—have. They thus become a pretext for
venturesome speculations in which we can no longer clearly
discern what the missionary is to bring to the Gentiles—nor
even what remains of the treasure entrusted to him.

Père Teilhard was a true believer. He was fully aware of the
unique reality of the Incarnation, and the *unique* freshness of
the Christian message, and "the *unique* power of divinization"
placed by the Spirit of Christ in his *unique* Church—hence he
avoided this danger. In his eyes, it was "the Christian Mystique," and not some other, which was to become "the universal
and essential Mystique of the future." [93] He knew that to illu-
minate human life there exists a Truth that has "come down
from heaven," which is of another order from those truths dis-

covered by men[94]—and that there is no serious dialogue without a confrontation. He believed and proclaimed that "without the Church, Christ vanishes, or crumbles, or is nullified," and he acknowledged Rome as "the Christic pole of the earth." [95]

His ideal of "integralism" (which, like Blondel, he opposed to "integrism") consisted in "the extension of Christian directives to the totality of resources contained in the world." [96] Though he desired that Christianity "should open her axes to embrace in its totality the new pulsation of religious energy which rises from below to be sublimated," he knew that this great effort of integration, sublimation, and synthesis must be achieved "without modifying the position at its summit," that is to say, without impairing its revealed mystery.[97]

He also understood that in order to be integrated, as he said, into "the Christian phylum," or to be ingrafted "on the Roman stock" (we might point out that this image came from his scientific vocabulary as well as from the Epistle to the Romans), the spiritual acquisitions of humanity need to be purified, oriented, transformed, "converted." [98] He said this both with respect to ancient acquisitions, preserved in the various religious systems, as well as with respect to the new acquisitions that result from the present development of our species. Neither did he doubt the "extraordinary power of Christianity" to achieve this:

> Far from losing its primacy in the vortex of the vast religious conflict unleashed by the totalization of the modern world, Christianity on the contrary resumes and consolidates its axial and directing place at the head of the psychical human energies, provided that sufficient attention is paid to its extraordinary and significant power of "pan-amorization." [99]

Neither did Teilhard fail to understand the gravity of refusing God to whom man is ever exposed, nor the exigencies of "segregation," correlative to personal "aggregation" to the Body of Christ; this is what renders our history—until the very hour of the Parousia—always so dramatic. And no more than he conducted himself in the least as a "member of the underground" with regard to those who represented God's authority for him, did he bear the slightest disdain toward the faith of simple souls, as long as it was sincere. He even yearned to match it exactly in order to remain faithful with all of them "in conformity with the spirit and living tradition of the Church"; hence, he always formally added on to his most personal views, those which might be regarded as the most disputable, the phrase: "without attenuation of the Christian tradition." [100] (He was to write the same words two days before his death.)

We will not maintain that he fully succeeded in his effort of systematization; but this was his constant desire, his effective orientation—and such is the criterion to which he himself wished his thought ultimately to be submitted. In his optimism he did not conceive of illusory "human hopes" without relation to "the Christian hope": his passionate interest in man's work on this earth—far from diverting his thought from the hereafter—drew all its vigor from the latter and in fact was completely ordered by it.[101]

Finally, in his perpetual dialogue with the unbeliever, he certainly took care to trace "a comprehensible way" for him, and to lead him to it through suitable stages—but it was always a way leading to Jesus Christ.[102] He was consumed by a Fire that he strove to propagate.

In all this Père Teilhard de Chardin resembled every other apostle-disciple of the great Apostle. But the greatness of his personality possibly renders his example more significant, and perhaps it is also more particularly opportune to remind everyone of this today. Whatever (even grave) adhesions or reservations may ultimately be elicited in a reader of Teilhard by one or other stage of the itinerary he traces, one thing is indisputable: the purpose that he assigns to the human adventure is the same as the Gospel's. It is a purpose that can be attained only by sacrificing—through the medium of death—every element of this world, but which already commences becoming manifest to us, amid all our travails and all our pains, in the "joy of adoration." [103]

PART TWO

FROM THE WORLD TO GOD
AND CHRIST
IN THE WORK OF
TEILHARD DE
CHARDIN

Introduction

Under one of its principal aspects, the entire work of Père Teilhard de Chardin can be regarded as one vast proof—renewed in a scientific perspective—for the immortality of the human soul and the existence of God; a proof that is completed by a preparatory effort reaching to the threshold of the Christian faith. In any case, such was one of the constant projects of its author. This is evident from his numerous personal statements as well as from an examination of his writings. Furthermore, it appears very early.

The outlines of such a view are already drawn, for example, in the capital study concerned with *Hominization,* first draft of subsequent studies on the *Phenomenon of Man,* dated May 6, 1923.[1] However, it is elaborated in more detail only from about 1930 onward: first in *l'Esprit de la Terre* [*The Spirit of the Earth*] (1931) and later in the series of analogous memoirs that followed at brief intervals,[2] notably in *Comment je crois* [*How I Believe*] (1934). A simple glance at the subtitles of this last opuscule[3] will immediately bear this out.

To illustrate this basic plan, we will choose the summary—among many others—found in a text dated October 9, 1936 from Peking, which was drawn up at the wish of the Roman Congregation for the Propagation of the Faith upon request of the apostolic delegate in China: *Quelques réflexions sur la conversion du monde* [*Some Reflections on the Conversion of the World*]. It outlines a program which in Père Teilhard de Char-

41

din's view is to be realized in three stages, or by three successive steps—philosophical, dogmatic, and moral:

A first step would consist in developing (along the lines of the *"perennial philosophy"*: primacy of being, act, and potency:) a correct physics and metaphysics of evolution. I am convinced that an honest interpretation of the new achievements of scientific thought justifiably leads not to a materialistic but to a spiritualistic interpretation of evolution:—the world we know is not developing by chance, but is structurally controlled by a personal Center of universal convergence.[4]

We will refrain from going into the details of the argument itself. This would require a lengthy study involving the whole of Teilhardian thought. Furthermore, Père Teilhard de Chardin's views are varied, and the exposition of each has more than once also varied at least in its nuances of expression, in accord with the viewpoints adopted and the interlocutors successively envisaged by the author in the course of his existence.[5]

Similarly, we will not institute a critical examination of these views nor will we take them as such into account. We merely wish to designate their orientation and extract its principal moments, considering them so to speak from the outside. Such a procedure is somewhat similar to the way in which Père Teilhard was accustomed to consider man himself, as an objective phenomenon, so that he might note the most general characteristics.

The "Initial Postulate"

At the start Père Teilhard habitually asks that something be granted—some single point: this is what he terms a "postulate," or a "fundamental option" in favor of existence, or of the goodness of existence, the value of existence; sometimes he also says:

"faith in the world," in the goodness of the world. Such an initial request is dictated by the experience of his contacts with certain unbelievers. Some are ready from the outset to grant this postulate, which thus provides a common ground for further research. But others are more recalcitrant. On May 11, 1923 he wrote from a ship taking him to China, "between Saigon and Hong Kong":

Last night I had a long talk with the Doctor and another passenger on questions of moral philosophy. We finally had to admit that we differed on such fundamentals as: "Is it better to be or not?"
I believe, in fact, that this is a fundamental option of all thought, a postulate which cannot be proved but from which everything is deduced. Once it is admitted that being is better than its opposite, it is difficult to stop short of God; if it is not admitted, discussion ceases to be possible.[6]

This lesson was not lost. In a few of his writings, Père Teilhard is anxious to alert his reader in formal fashion: "No reflective construction would be possible without the initial choice which makes us incline heart and mind for existence rather than non-existence";[7] or again: " 'Is the state of being good or bad? That is to say, is it better to be than not to be?' Despite its abstract, metaphysical form, this is essentially a practical question representing the fundamental dilemma upon which every man is compelled to pronounce, implicitly or explicitly, by the very fact of having been born." [8]

"Faith in existence," or "faith in the world": this is still—at least apparently—nothing more than a starting point. But gradually this initial faith (whose nature is to be made precise) will necessarily lead to faith "in some ultimate consummation of *everything* that surrounds us." [9] Its content will be revealed only little by little: yet in reality it is already in a sense all-inclusive. Indeed, in the measure that the proof will develop, the "initial faith" used as a starting point will undergo a series of enlargements, precisions, explications or mutations ("meltings"). Thus at the end of a chain of reasoning the person who had "stayed with" Teilhard could say with him that he now believed "in the ultimate (rather than primary) goodness and value of things":[10] for they will henceforth appear to him to be rooted in God.

This is what Pastor Georges Crespy has noted in his thesis concerning Teilhard's thought in *La Pensée théologique de Teilhard de Chardin* [*The Theological Thought of Teilhard de Chardin*] when analyzing the opuscule entitled *Comment je crois* [*How I Believe*] which commences with a profession of "faith in the world." "Teilhard," he concludes, "has the courage to trust his initial intuitions to the very end; he has secretly foreseen that the terminus will justify everything." [11]

The "Third Abyss"

The existence which we share and in which we are immersed even before having begun to think or to act presents itself to us from the outset as an evolution. This is, in Père Teilhard de Chardin's view, more than a scientific conception; in the aftermath of the progress of science, it is an acquisition of consciousness, and its perception—though still confused—will become more and more evident.[12] Accordingly, his entire concern is to establish that such an evolution does not happen "by chance." Whoever takes the time to unravel it will find it intelligible; it reveals a meaning because it has a meaning in itself. Its signification lies in its direction. It terminates in man and consequently man is the key to the universe.

The tradition of spiritualistic philosophy, particularly in its Christian form, made man "the king of creation." Furthermore, in the opinion of a number of modern thinkers this tradition was entirely connected with the static representations of the ancient cosmology: when the latter fall, so do the former. At the time

Père Teilhard was just beginning to write, a work was enjoying huge success popularizing this theme: *Les affirmations de la conscience moderne* [*The Affirmations of the Modern Conscience*] by Gabriel Séailles.[13] And it continues to remain the opinion of a considerable number of scholars today who find supporters among many philosophers with little sympathy for cosmology.

Teilhard does not attempt to defend an ancient position against them by means of a defensive apologetics in the nature of a rearguard action. He undertakes to show scientifically not only that the ancient tradition is not superseded by the advent of a new age, but that it must be considered to be even more solidly established—although under an entirely new form. The evolution he sets forth is one "grand orthogenesis of everything living towards a higher degree of spontaneity." [14]

Through the increasing complexity of organisms and finally of the nervous system this is a "rise of consciousness": such is the way in which the axis of "cosmogenesis" can be defined.[15] Pascal's two infinites, the two abysses of greatness and inferiority, must not only be supplemented but opposed by a third which reverses the whole situation: the infinite of complexity.[16] This "third abyss" which is the "abyss of synthesis" [17] succeeds in burrowing itself in man in whom evolution finally becomes conscious of itself:[18] "In the human spirit, as in some unique and irreplaceable fruit we find gathered together the whole sublimity of life, that is, the entire cosmic value of the earth." [19]

Teilhard goes on to conclude: "In fact, I doubt whether there is a more decisive moment for a thinking being than when the scales fall from his eyes and he discovers that he is not an isolated unit lost in the cosmic solitudes, and realizes that a universal will to live converges and is hominized in him":[20]

Since Galileo (as Freud remarked), in the eyes of science, man has continually lost, one after another, the privileges that had previously made him consider himself unique in the world.

Astronomically, first of all (like and with the earth) he was engulfed in the enormous anonymity of the stellar bodies; then *biologically,* when like every other animal he vanished in the crowd of his fellow-species; *psychologically,* last of all when an abyss of unconsciousness opened in the center of his *I;* by three successive steps in four centuries, man, I repeat, has seemed definitely to redissolve in the common ground of things.

Now, paradoxically, this same man is in the process of re-emerging from his return to the crucible, more than ever *at the head of nature;* since by his very melting back into the general current of convergent cosmogenesis, he is acquiring in our eyes the possibility and power of forming himself in the heart of space and time, *a single point of universalization* for the very stuff of the world . . .[21]

Pascal and Voltaire—for once in agreement as it has been observed—regarded man as crushed by the universe. Pascal salvaged the dignity of man by concentrating on thought, something that a certain number of our contemporaries no longer can do. However, by this consideration, he did not save man: all that he salvaged for man in the final analysis was the knowledge that he is crushed by the universe whereas "the universe has no knowledge of the advantage the universe has over him." [22]

"What is one man in infinity?" The real superiority of this man and his victory over the blind forces of the universe were only really reestablished by faith. For Pascal had just assisted at the collapse of the ancient cosmology: "The eternal silence of these infinite spaces frightens me."

From the time of Pascal and Voltaire, science has progressed; after space it has discovered time (duration); the collapse of the ancient cosmology has been carried to its ultimate extent and man has appeared even more lost, if such were possible, in the depths of the universe.[23] Once again "a properly revolutionary scientific advance subverts the idea that man forms himself out of himself and his situation in the world"; once more "by means of this revolution doubt is cast upon the confidence that the spirit has in the spirit." [24]

It is then that Teilhard—by positing the infinite of complexity as the term of cosmic evolution—reestablishes man with one and the same stroke not only in his dignity but in his effective domination as well. He rightly discerns that "the universe is an immense thing wherein we should be lost if it did not converge on a Person";[25] but all his effort culminates precisely in the establishment of such convergence.

Did he fully establish it? Pascal saw "only infinities on all sides," which hemmed him in "like an atom and like a shadow which lasts only for an instant and never returns"; the universe he described was a world that had "lost all its structure."[26] Was Teilhard able—by scrutinizing the laws of evolution—to give a structure to this world? Is his theory of hominization absolutely proven, at least in its essential lines? It would be well worth examining seriously. At least, it is impossible to act—in judging him—as if he had never attempted a proof.

We will simply state here that Pascal and Voltaire have nothing to say to us against this theory. For neither Pascal nor Voltaire knew "the new crisis of the spirit" which Teilhard wished to confront and neither Pascal nor Voltaire could have foreseen "the change in perspective" thanks to which Teilhard believed it possible to conclude that "there is henceforth in our eyes a past and a future, that is to say, a growth of the world."[27]

"The Rise of the Spirit"

In the Teilhardian universe, cosmogenesis terminates in anthropogenesis.[28] Hence, the cosmological proof for the existence of God which Teilhard goes on to construct on this foundation can just as well be termed an anthropological proof—just as well and even more. For it proceeds through man, through the spirit of man, which is the "spirit of the earth."

We must not take this last expression, or similar expressions, to mean that spirit is a product of matter. This would be a gross misunderstanding. For Teilhard the evolutionary perspective has renewed the manner of understanding the classic distinction between matter and spirit: it has in no wise abolished such a distinction. If he has at times been misunderstood, the reason is that a metaphysical signification has been attached from the outset to explanations given on the phenomenal plane.

Yet Père Teilhard never stopped explaining himself. Already in November 1917, he wrote: "Properly understood, consciousness must not be regarded as a simple resultant. . . . [It is] the appearance in the world of something entirely new. . . . [It is] a new substance." [29] "The unifying force of the multiple, the spirit cannot be composed of the multiple." It appears "to be charged with the remains of matter," but not made from matter. It arises experimentally "in matter which is more and more synthesized," but this does not signifiy that matter without anything added changes itself into spirit.

From one to the other there exists a whole complex network of "liaisons" and "oppositions." Spirit is not matter any more than the "within" of things is their "without." Doubtless, matter and form are not like "two compartments" or "two things": such a dualism—far from assuring the existence of the spirit— would materialize it. Doubtless, too, the same being possesses a certain concrete unity of the "within" and the "without," matter and spirit. The remark has even been made with reference to Claude Bernard and Père Sertillanges, not Teilhard, "that this is what St. Thomas was basically teaching." [30]

It is no less certain for Teilhard that "all consciousness comes from the spirit" [31] or, what amounts to the same thing, that "if things hold and hold together, it is only by reason of complexity from above," [32] the materialism being only an illusion due to a "crass view of things"; or further, that "the sole stability of things is imparted to them by their synthetic [synthesizing] element, that is, by that which is their soul or spirit to a more or less perfect degree." [33]

But what is equally certain is that we constantly seek stability with reference to and starting from the material universe. For we reason using our senses as a starting point. We have no intuition of what is pure spirit. "No spirit (even God within the limits of our experience) exists or could exist, through construction, without a multiple which would be associated with it." [34] Put in another way—to use the language of our classic philosophy—it is only in virtue of the world that by a rational induction we can posit the existence of God. At first sight, this is true —with the necessary modifications—for every spirit.

The rise of the spirit (that is, of reflective consciousness and of freedom) beginning with matter, and synthesizing matter, is an *irreversible* ascent. This irreversibility is precisely what we call, and what Père Teilhard himself sometimes also calls, immortality.[35] In other words, in the cosmos at the end of cosmogenesis the victory of "convergence" over dispersing entropy, over "disintegration and universal desegregation" [36]—in short, victory of the spirit over matter—is assured.

Hence, Teilhard duplicates the classic idea of the immortality of each spiritual soul by that of a collective immortality. He duplicates it, but, we should note, he does not replace it. For "the spirit of the earth" has nothing about it of an undifferentiated collective reality: it is composed of personal spirits. The process of spiritualization is in effect identically a process of personalization; it terminates in "the incommunicable uniqueness of each reflective element," [37] and this is one of the ways in which the Teilhardian expression of "personal universe" must be understood. The irreversibility of the cosmos is thus in the final analysis the personal immortality of all the souls that compose it. Indeed, at its terminus, the cosmos in its very unity is essentially "a world of souls." [38]

A struggle is in progress "in the universe between the unified *multiple* and the unorganised *multitude*." [39] This is a grandiose duel that stretches over the length of cosmic evolution and will terminate with the decisive victory of the unified multiple, that is, of the personal Spirit. Père Teilhard described it in a succession of expositions repeated ceaselessly, with an effort at ever-increasing precision; for example in a 1951 essay on the convergence of the universe (*Convergence de l'Univers*):

A certain fundamental law (reveals itself to us) affecting the whole world. No longer is there in the universe, as we continue to repeat, only the disheartening entropy, inexorably reducing all things to the most elementary and most stable forms. Rather, through and above this shower of ashes, there emerges a kind of cosmic vortex, in whose center the stuff of the world—by the preferential utilization of chances—twists and unrolls more and more tightly within itself, in ever more complicated and centered assemblages.[40]

"Thus there reappears in Thought," after an eclipse which many believed was definitive, "that incorruptibility wherein the ancient philosophy justly discerned the most characteristic attribute of the spiritual." [41]

A Proof for God

Once we have established this irreversible convergence of the universe—or better, "the cosmic derivative of complexity-consciousness"—we reach the last link in the chain that terminates in the necessary affirmation of God.

For a point must be reached in which human consciousness is attained. "There lies before us . . . some critical and final point of ultra-hominization, corresponding to a complete reflection of the noosphere on itself";[42] we might add—to sum up lengthy explanations that have no direct bearing on our present perspective—a point of perfect personalization, in a unity which is the opposite of a homogeneous identity. A *processus in infinitum* [*process to infinity*] is impossible.

This achievement, or this "complete reflection," is the primary meaning which Père Teilhard attaches to what he calls the "Omega point." "Superior pole of human co-reflection," "summit of hominization," such a point is still immanent. But just as it was impossible to tend indefinitely toward it without ever attaining it, so is it equally impossible to remain at such a point. We see the demonstration of this in a page of the *Esquisse d'une dialectique de l'esprit* [*Sketch of a Dialectic of the Spirit*] (1946). Among the most varied forms that the proof for God's existence assumes in Teilhard, this is unquestionably at least the most systematic—if not the most technical; it is the one which flows most from his particular views concerning the future of man as elaborated by him especially in the second part of his career. Thus it is also—at least in our eyes—the form most subject to contestation:

The natural evolution of the biosphere is prolonged in what I have called the noosphere, but it assumes a clearly *convergent* form therein, designating toward the summit a *point of maturation* (or collective reflection). . . . (At this point) reflective humanity collectively remains alone before itself. In these circumstances it is impossible to imagine an ulterior complexification determining a superior consciousness. Our law of recurrence automatically ceases to function. . . . So that . . . man is seen drifting toward a terminal position in which:

a) organically, he cannot go any further (even collectively) in complexity, hence in consciousness;
b) psychically, he cannot accept falling back;
c) and cosmically, he cannot remain in one place, since in our "entropized" universe to cease advancing means to fall back.

What else can we say except that having arrived at this ultra-critical point of maturation, the curve of the human phenomenon pierces the cosmic phenomenal system and postulates the existence before and after of some extracosmic pole in which is found integrally collected and definitively consolidated the entire reflective incommunicable successively formed in the universe . . . in the course of evolution?[43]

Seen from below, from our vantage point, the apex of the evolutive cone (the point Omega) stands out on the horizon as a center of convergence, purely immanent—humanity engrossed in contemplating itself. But on closer study we realize that this center, in order to hold together, must have behind it, yet a more profound than it is, a transcendent nucleus—necessarily divine.[44]

As we have said, this is merely one of the forms of the Teilhardian argumentation. It supposes a vision of the future "extrapolated on the curve constructed with the data offered by actual observation." [45] For more than one reason a similar extrapolation, practiced with such boldness, could appear to be disputable;[46] and since in the judgment of Père Teilhard himself it is hardly more than "probable," [47] it does not without certainty constitute an entirely sufficient basis.

Teilhard returned to this point on several occasions, notably in *Man's Place in Nature;* after resuming the argumentation just outlined in more detail and with all possible rigor, he concludes in prudent and measured terms:

As things now stand, modern astronomers have no hesitation in envisaging the existence of a sort of primitive atom in which the entire mass of the sidereal world, if we took it back several thousands of millions of years, would be found. Matching in a way, this primordial physical unity, is it not odd that if biology is extrapolated to its extreme point (and this time ahead of us) it leads us to an analogous hypothesis: the hypothesis of a universal focus (I have called it Omega), no longer one of physical expansion and exteriorization but of psychic interiorization.[48]

But there are—as we have also noted—other and more simple forms of Teilhard's argumentation whose probative force appears more universal. Msgr. Bruno de Solages has summarized three of the main ones with his customary vigor and clarity, also indicating the passages which can be consulted to complete the exposition. He has designated them by the following names: (1) Proof through human action, or "the Absolute, postulate of Evolution";[49] (2) proof through efficient or ordaining causality, or "God, first Mover of ascending Evolution"; (3) proof through the aspirations of the human soul, or "God to be loved, condition of ultimate unification of the converging noosphere." [50]

Other commentators, such as Maurice Corvez, O.P.,[51] or C. Valverde Mucientes, S.J.,[52] distinguish these proofs in a slightly different manner. Furthermore, even in the thought of their author, they are not adequately distinct from one another.

What Père Teilhard wished primarily to demonstrate through all of these to our contemporaries and what we draw out of all this was expressed by him in his 1945 work *Action et Activation:* "The problem of a prime Mover and an antecedent last Collector does not diminish; on the contrary, it increases in importance and urgency with the formidable accretions imposed by science on our representations of the universe." [53]

And it was in direct confrontation with this problem that he was anxious to place and leave his auditors or readers, even when the subject treated might appear to be chiefly concerned with pure science. Here we have then the example of the last page of *Man's Place in Nature,* a résumé of the lectures given at the Sorbonne in the course of the winter of 1949–1950 "for advanced students" [54] in which he set forth in particularly technical terms a condensation of his vision of the universe.

Unless it is to be powerless to form the keystone of the noosphere, "Omega" can only be conceived as the *meeting-point* between a universe that has reached the limit of centration, and *another,* even deeper *center*—this being the self-subsistent center and absolutely final Principle of irreversibility and personalization: the one and only true Omega. And it is at this point, if I am not mistaken, in the science of evolution . . . , that the problem of God comes in—Prime Mover, Gatherer and Consolidater, ahead of us, of evolution.[55]

The Attributes of Omega

Some attributes of this divine Omega, "the one and only true Omega," are already enumerated in the preceding texts. Doubtless, such a "Center," such a "Pole," such a "Focus," "in itself and by definition is not directly comprehensible to us": for it is a question of an "extracosmic energy in its origin (although immanent in its term)." [56] Hence, the analysis of the evolutive movement and its requirement of intelligibility does not suffice in enabling us to penetrate "the divine nature of Omega"; but it does allow us to formulate a few conditions which it must meet in order to fulfill its role.[57]

The first of these conditions, or the first attribute of Omega, to be noted is its very reality, or its actuality: "Neither an ideal center, nor a potential center could possibly suffice. A present and real noosphere goes with a real and present center. To be supremely attractive, Omega must be supremely present." [58] It incorporates a "mastery over time and chance," alone capable of furnishing a guarantee of success to our spirit. It is, as we have seen, "a First Mover and a Last Collector," or in other words, "Alpha and Omega at the same time, sole Origin, sole Issue, sole Term." [59] This "First Being" is of absolute necessity a "personal" or "ultra-personal Being," since it is a "personalizing Focus." [60] It is a "real Pole of convergence," "a Center different from all Centers, which it 'super-centers' in assimilating them, a Person distinct from all the persons whom it completes in unifying." [61]

This is for Teilhard a very important affirmation to which he continually returns: "A world presumed to be heading towards the Impersonal . . . becomes both unthinkable and unliveable," [62] and "the personal elements of the universe would return to disorder (that is, to nothing) if they did not encounter an already actualized Supra-Personal Being to dominate them. Hence, to equilibrate our action, there must be found in the world around us not only the hope but even the recognizable visage of a universal Personality." [63] In other words, we must posit a "supremely personal [God], from whom we are the more distinct the more we lose ourselves in him." [64] Consequently, as the "last Center" Omega must be conceived as a "supreme Personality." It is "a summit of transcendence," a "primordial transcendence," "a transcendent Reality." [65] In short, "autonomy, actuality, irreversibility, and thus finally transcendence are the four attributes of Omega." [66]

This fourth attribute, which discourages us beforehand from clothing "the intimate nature of Omega" in a rational definition, nevertheless does not leave us in pure nescience with regard to this subject. This Being who is "not only at the head of all series, but . . . in some way outside any series," this Being who alone "finds in himself his proper stability," [67] is a mysterious Being. He "does not offer himself to our finite beings as a thing all complete and ready to be embraced," but "for us he is eternal discovery and eternal growth. The more we think we understand him, the more he reveals himself as otherwise. The more we think we hold him, the further he withdraws, drawing us into the depths of himself." [68]

It will be noted that at one time or another Père Teilhard de Chardin affirms that the Omega point is "partially transcendent, that is, practically independent of the evolution that culminates in it." He thus reunites or rather considers still united, according to the logic of the discovery, the two significations that he successively acknowledged for this word Omega.

In other words, he is thus speaking not of God alone nor of the world alone, but of "their meeting point"; and he cannot forget—due to proper method—that it is *primarily* the unified world, the world arrived at its term, that he has naturally designated by this symbolic appellation. The continuation of the text from which we have taken the preceding words brings this out very clearly.

For we are told, "If Omega would not in some way escape from the conditions of time and space, it could neither be already present to us, nor would it be capable . . . of establishing the hopes of irreversibility without which—beginning with man—centrogenesis would cease to function. Thus it is that through a face of itself [its divine face, God] different from the one under which we see it developing [= its cosmic and human face, 'immanent' Omega], it eternally emerges over a world from which however it is in the process of emerging under another aspect. . . ." [69]

Put still another way, this complex Omega, at the end of the argumentation that would take its starting point in the observation of the cosmos in process of unification, would appear as "a centered system of centers, but" itself centered on "a Center of centers." "The Center of superior order," it "waits for us— already it seems—no longer beside us but also *apart* and *above* us." [70]

And if we had set forth some other aspects of the Teilhardian proof, it would be more apparent that the actuality of Omega is the actuality of Love; that its personality is the personality of Love; that its power of attraction is the power of Love; finally, that Omega is Love itself at once "lovable and loving." [71]

Reason and Revelation

We have already seen in several places and again in the passages just cited, that the necessity of positing the existence of God starting from the observation of the world in convergent evolution refers in Père Teilhard's eyes principally—yet not uniquely—to the necessity of positing a unifying Being. It is chiefly in his unifying function that God is attained. [72]

The Christian Revelation teaches us on the other hand that God created the world in a loving thought, in order to unite it to himself; that the realization of this divine plan is effected by the Incarnation, and that it is by our union achieved in Christ (mystical Body) that each of us is united with God.

Père Teilhard always professed a strict idea of Revelation, understood in its twofold character: intellectual (which does not exclude the affective) and supernatural. He knows that it is "an affirmation from on high" and culminates in "the fact of the Incarnation." [73] Accordingly, when he states in *le Christique* [*The Christic*] (1965): "In the final analysis, cosmogenesis after discovering itself, following its principal axis biogenesis, then noogenesis, culminates in the Christogenesis revered by all Christians," he does not intend to suggest that this passage in our spirit from noogenesis to Christogenesis was effected by a natural dialectic.

Certain abbreviated expositions in which he places himself immediately at the viewpoint of the faith might have led a few commentators astray. However, as Madame M. Barthélemy-Madaule has observed, "it is often we," in our summaries of his thought, "who intermingle the [various] levels, who too often effect not a synthesis but a mélange, and are then astonished by the confusion." [74]

Père Teilhard himself criticized those who he said "naively" confuse "the planes of the real," and who for example make Christ "a physical agent *of the same order* as organic life or the ether"; this was in his eyes "both reprehensible and laughable." [75] He was accustomed to distinguish clearly between the two spheres of what he called the "heavenly truth" and the "earthly truth," or "that which is taught" and "that which is discovered," or further "the divine sphere" and "the cosmic sphere."

To appreciate this, we need only observe the composition of a certain number of his writings; how, for example, he introduces the "phenomenon of man," whether in the *Phenomenon of Man* itself or in [*The Singularities of the Human Species*]; or further, how he appeals to "the Christian mystique" toward the end of his *Réflexions sur le bonheur* [*Reflections on Happiness*] or once more, how in the second part of *Comment je crois* [*How I Believe*] he departs from the ways of individual experience and rational demonstration in order to interrogate history.

To describe this divine revelation, he spoke of "Omega seeing itself, *revealing* itself, affectively and intelligibly, on the reflective surface of the noosphere." [76] With greater precision, he wrote: "The entire value of Christianity, all its power to uplift souls, calls for its presentation as Something *imposed* from above, as the Other . . . , already *actuated,* constituted *extra nos* [outside ourselves]: such is the essence of the idea of Revelation." [77]

But he also states: "The Christian need merely meditate on his *Credo* to find in the Revelation which he admits the unhoped-for realization of the dream at whose threshold he is logically conducted by philosophy." [78]

For he knows that the reality of Christ cannot in any way be *deduced* from the world, but he also knows that Revelation consolidates, prolongs, and completes the work sketched out by reason. He joyfully discovers a "remarkable similarity" between dogmatic perspectives and the conclusions or ultimate hypotheses to which he is led by the study of the phenomenon of man, a similarity which he rightly attributes to the "influence" and "radiance" of the Christian Revelation. If there is discontinuity, distinction, and hierarchy between reason and faith just as between nature and grace, there is just as much harmony. Teilhard insists—at times no doubt to excess—on the second of these two aspects, but without really misunderstanding the first.

The Omega Christ

"In every hypothesis, the world demands to be centered in order to be thinkable." However, it could be such in many more or less imperfect ways, which are difficult for us to imagine now-adays. "What precisely constitutes the 'generous' character of the present world is that the place of the universal Center has not been accorded to some supreme intermediary between God and the universe"—which accordingly would not have obtained per-fect "centrality"—"but is occupied by the Godhead itself, which thus introduces us . . . into the . . . bosom of its imma-nence." [79]

In other words, "instead of the vague center of convergence envisaged as the ultimate end of this process of evolution, the personal and defined reality of the Word incarnate, in which everything acquires substance, appears and takes its place." [80] "Naturally," then, there is "only the expectation for a unifica-tion: without Christ, the cosmos would have no natural Omega; it would remain open"; but in our present situation, "the Incar-nation has so thoroughly *recentered* the universe within the supernatural that, in the *concrete,* we can no longer seek to imagine toward what center the elements of this world would have gravitated, had they not been elevated to the order of grace." [81]

This gives rise to the Teilhardian formula: "The revealed Christ is nothing other than Omega," [82] or to analogous for-mulas. The welding of the natural order to the supernatural order, has taken place. "Under the illuminating influence of grace, our spirit recognizes in the unitive properties of the Chris-tian phenomenon a manifestation (reflection) of Omega on the human consciousness, and it identifies the Omega of reason with the universal Christ of Revelation." [83]

After citing his favorite Pauline texts: "In eo omnia constant" ["In him all things hold together"] (Col. 1, 17); "Ipse est qui replet omnia" ["He fills all things"] (Col. 2, 10; cf. Eph. 4, 9); "Omnia in omnibus Christus" ["Christ is all things to all"] (Col. 3, 11), Père Teilhard can exclaim: "This is the very definition of Omega." Jesus, the Word made flesh, dead and arisen, has become "the universal Christ." He is the one who gives stability to all things, who unites all things and influences all of them "physically" (with the precisions we shall see later on). The universe is "Christified."

"Through the Incarnation God descends into nature to superanimate it and unite it to himself. . . . In itself this dogma can be accommodated to widely divergent representations of the experimental world." The Christian has never encountered difficulty in thinking of it in terms of a static universe, and Père Teilhard de Chardin was not so naive as to imagine that a St. Paul or a St. John would have had an advance conception of universal evolution; he was not so bold as to think that by conceiving this himself he obtained a more profound view of the mystery than theirs.

But, what he did have evidence of was that in a universe as conceived by materialistic evolution "Christianity would have been snuffed out." Now, humanly speaking, the risk had become serious; it was imminent. "In the eyes of man, a universe *in genesis* was irresistibly replacing the static universe of theologians. In turn, this new intuition also inevitably gave rise to a special mystique: a more or less adulatory faith in the terrestrial and cosmic future of evolution. . . . Once the universe was set in motion, a kind of Divinity, entirely immanent in the world, tended progressively to be substituted in the human mind for the transcendent Christian God. . . ."

This was the reason for Père Teilhard's undertaking, an undertaking in whose wake he can seemingly ask with reason: Though itself not dependent on any one of our representations or scientific hypotheses, does not the dogma of the Incarnation "find its most suitable environment in the . . . perspectives . . . of a universe directed by the Spirit?" [84]

We can now better understand the meaning and the interest of the text already cited:

Under the illuminating influence of grace, our spirit recognizes in the unitive properties of the Christian phenomenon a manifestation (reflection) of Omega on the human consciousness, and it identifies the Omega of reason with the universal Christ of Revelation." [85]

Père Teilhard thus believed that a Transformism more seriously studied and understood would reveal itself "capable of forming an excellent basis for Christian thought and action." [86]

Not only does the Christological tradition through experience show itself capable of tolerating an evolutionary structure of the world; but even more, contrary to all previews, it is at the heart of this new organic and unitary milieu, in favor of this particular orientation of space linked with time, that it develops most freely and fully. It is there that it assumes its true form. . . . Christianity and evolution are not two irreconcilable visions, but two perspectives destined to fit together and complement each other.[87]

Here, already, in the satisfaction of having wholly reversed a critical situation, the apologist lets himself be carried away to some excess, contrary to the measured statements that he had at first uttered. Nevertheless, at least one thing appears very certain. Understood as explained by Père Teilhard, such a formula as the one that ultimately the Christ of Revelation is merely the Omega of evolution not only presents nothing disquieting or even, to tell the truth, paradoxical, but also, instead of admitting some untenable system of "double truth," it imposes itself. The Omega of the *Book of Revelation* and that of evolution cannot be two distinct and rival summits.

It is really the Omega discovered in its transcendence at the conclusion of the rational quest—and not some other—which the Christian can characterize in the light of his faith as having or being a "trinitarian focus." There is only one God. The God of faith cannot be really different from the God of reason. The God of Abraham, Isaac, and Jacob may not be "the God of philosophers and scientists": but he is in any case the same as the God of science and philosophy.

From Science to Philosophy

Among the characteristics of the Teilhardian proofs for the existence of God we will cite two in particular.

First of all, we must realize that these are intended to be scientific proofs. To establish the nature of evolution, the superiority of man, the progress of the world toward the spirit, the terminal convergence, etc., Père Teilhard de Chardin constantly refers and wishes to refer uniquely to an "experimental law of recurrence, verifiable in the phenomenal sphere, and conveniently extrapolated on the totality of space and time." This law of recurrence suffices, he claims, for it "presides at the formation of beings"; and it is according to this law that "the cosmos is constructed." [88]

He discards every "*a priori* geometric synthesis, starting from some definition of 'being,' " and adheres "strictly to the examination and arrangement of appearances, that is 'phenomenona.' " Despite a few excesses here and there in the presentation of his method—for example, when he states that he is restricting himself expressly "to the area of facts, that is, the domain of the tangible and the photographable"—he is nevertheless well aware that his science, or as he says his phenomenology, which links synthesis to analysis and posits a "without" of things, transcends the concept of "positive science" currently in vogue.

It approaches, he himself explains, the "Physics" of the ancient Greeks, and the Medievalists. Although he does not enter the paths of an "abstract metaphysics," he intends very much to seek a "physics of the spirit," an "ultra-physics of the universe." [89] And he sees perfectly well that it terminates accordingly in the "exact reversal of the present world of science." [90]

Concerning this point a certain number of interrelated questions can arise:

1) To what extent is it legitimate to introduce synthesis into a science which desires to be exact?

2) Can there be a scientific proof for God? If such is claimed, does this not entail reverting to the "confusionism" which according to some characterized the rational efforts of the great medieval theologians starting with St. Thomas?

3) Nevertheless, in virtue of his conception of an evolving and converging universe did not Père Teilhard precisely discover a new and legitimate way for passing from science to philosophy? In other words, did he not succeed—not only through a mystic view but through a properly rational view—in lifting the "veil of phenomena," in tearing down "the impermeable membrane that the phenomenon stretches between us and all that is above the human spirit?" [91]

We will leave these questions unanswered. It would be impossible to answer them in depth without raising all kinds of methodological problems into which we cannot go here. Furthermore, the third question would also require a profound examination of the whole of Teilhard's thought. We will merely cite three opinions closely corresponding to the three questions raised.[92]

Teilhard, states Père Norbert M. Luyten, O.P., "has transcended the methodological frameworks in which both the sciences and philosophy seemed to be enclosed";[93] expecting "little from an ever more extended *detailed research*," he realized very early that "in order to advance science and prevent it from petering out . . . , its object *must be enlarged* and *its methods changed,* and a *more profound and more synthetic study* attained." If he made use at times of "defective methodological procedures," he still had the merit "of providing us with indications of the greatest interest for the future of science, if only by posing in crude fashion the problem of a synthesis of our knowledge." [94]

Another Dominican, Père Maurice Corvez, is also not in the least daunted by the idea of a "scientific proof" for God: "With a superior mastery, Père Teilhard has paved a way of access to Christianity especially adapted to a category of scientists, geologists, paleontologists, biologists, but also most practicable for those interested in the history of nature and life, that is to say, all who are endowed with an authentic general culture." [95]

Finally, Madame Barthélemy-Madaule: "It must be agreed that our ancient categories are too rigid to express this slow maturation, this moment in which—on a plane that remains still phenomenal—a sense is in the process of emerging which is already philosophic." [96]

Indeed it may well be that by the rigorous application of his phenomenological method to the description of our universe, Teilhard has succeeded in breaking through "the magic circle of phenomenalism which, we are told, would invincibly limit our gaze toward a horizon of finite radius":

How much has been said even recently about our powerlessness to penetrate . . . beyond the primitive vision shared by the earliest human minds; that is to say, the impossibility of our advancing a step towards the direct or indirect perception of all that is hidden behind the veil of tangible experience! But it is just this supposedly impenetrable envelope of pure "phenomenon" which the rebounding thrust of human evolution pierces, at least at one point, since by its nature it is irreversible.

This does not mean that we can see what lies beyond and behind that trans-phenomenal zone of which we now have an inkling, any more than, having discerned the shape of the earth, we can foresee the landscape lying beyond the horizon. But at least we know that something exists beyond the circle which restricts our view, something into which we shall eventually emerge. It is enough to ensure that we no longer feel imprisoned.[97]

Yet we must admit that Père Teilhard himself has scarcely explained in his principles if not in his applications the method which would demonstrate the real basis of this result.

The Teilhardian Optimism

The second characteristic will detain us a little longer.

By supposing, as we have seen, right from the starting point, a faith in the value of existence, Père Teilhard supposes the indissoluble unity of the three notions of existence, truth, and value. This is very close to the equivalent of the three transcendentals of the scholastic theory: *ens, verum, bonum* [being, truth, goodness] (the idea of value able to unite in itself the good and the beautiful, which is too often neglected). Herein lies a foremost aspect of that fundamental optimism which all agree in recognizing in the Teilhardian thought, either to praise or to censure it; we will view it only in the two aspects under which it presents itself in our subject.[98]

Under the aspect which we have just cited, the Teilhardian optimism, we might note, is simply mingled with the refusal of the absurd. He himself warns us of this. If he uses the word "faith," it is as he goes on to explain in a completely analogical sense,[99] and because in fact experience has shown him that it is always possible for man, free of implicitly contradicting himself by the same, to refuse his trust in reason and to believe that reality is basically "absurd" and "repugnant"; reason itself, in its spontaneous usage, is less reluctant to accept total absurdity than such strictly circumscribed partial absurdity.

However, Père Teilhard equally maintains that, "under its most muffled form," this "initial faith is sensibly no different from compliance with a scientific truth," [100] although the temptation may be strong at certain moments to abandon it by giving

in to light-headedness.[101] He also observes—what would appear
to constitute a better expression of the same idea—that without
such a faith "the world, by becoming rational would logically
return to dust." [102]

When Père Teilhard de Chardin returned to Paris from China
in 1945 at the end of the last world war, he reacted very strongly
against the pessimistic and atheistic existentialist wave which
was then engulfing Europe. In several debates he—to use
Pascal's words—"stiffened against them." It is in great part from
this fact that a simplistic legend was created about him, even
before his work was really known. Since then the idea has been
propagated of a certain "Teilhardism," characterized by an easy
optimism.

However, this is not even a caricature; it is a falsification. For
Père Teilhard de Chardin, an easy optimism is not only naiveté,
inexperience, or foolishness; it is a sin.[103] He waged a struggle
against the myths which projected "a golden age" in the future.
Against pessimists or the "weary," against the bon vivants or
"pleasure-seekers" he sought not "optimists" but "zealots." [104]

In fact, he foresaw for humanity even more "violent interior
conflicts than those known to us." He believed that a universe
such as the one conceived by him, "in process of conscious concentration . . . , is precisely the one which must more naturally
and more necessarily suffer." [105] He professed that suffering
"grows in quantity and sharpness to the same rhythm as the rise
in consciousness through the ages." He further proclaimed that
"moral effort is necessarily accompanied by sacrifice," that "the
highest life is attained through death," that "perfection is tied in
with suffering," that there is "no progress in being without some
mysterious tribute of tears, blood, and sin"; and he received from
his faith—in order to live it with intensity—the teaching that all
the "prodigious spiritual energy" of Christianity "is born of the
cross." [106]

Without the soul's adhesion to "the already recognizable

visage of a Universal Personality," he believed it impossible "to preserve from fatal misdirection the powers accumulated at the heart of the individual, of societies, and of the world itself." [107] In the company of "worshipers of progress," he seemed "to be suffocating under an excessively low sky" and he used to say he experienced "a sensation of asphyxiation." [108] He never ceased to speak about the horror of a "closed world," the dreadful solitude of a humanity that would be unified without God, "the essential fear of the reflective element confronted by a Whole that was apparently blind," and the despair of feeling oneself shut in "by the cosmic Bubble"—from the time of *La Grande Monade* [*The Grand Monad*] (1918) until the time of *The End of the Species* (1952) and *La Barrière de la Mort* [*The Barrier of Death*] (1955).

He himself keenly felt human anguish—both that of all time and in particular that of our time; it is present throughout at the basis of his work and often even levels it off.[109] Only, instead of burying himself in it, complaining about it, or being content to groan under it, he sought to overcome it in a rational and Christian manner. Realizing that modern man in spite of all his science and all his powers is "sad," he wished to free him from this sadness. He undertook to "preserve the thinking earth from the *taedium vitae* [the tedium of life]" [110] and to work in us a "reversal of fear." [111]

As for his basic optimism, fruit of his "fundamental choice" for being, this optimism which says "yes" to creation, thus ratifying "the primordial choice implicated in the world whose reflective elements we are," [112] we might compare it justly enough to that of a St. Thomas Aquinas. In both cases, this optimism is related to a certain "zest for existence" which before influencing their doctrine characterizes their basic personality.[113] In virtue of this trait as well as a good many others, the thought of Père Teilhard de Chardin deserves to be classified in the line of Thomistic thought—more so than is yet customarily believed.[114]

And this zest—still natural—for existence was to be transformed and disappear in his prayer into a "zest for Being," "a profound zest" "a sentiment that Being is infinitely richer and more renewing than our logic," which in the very time of trial kept him in joy.[115]

However, would it not on the other hand be a very great optimism—and highly disputable—to believe as Père Teilhard did that the triumph of spirit over entropy is assured? This is the second aspect to be envisaged.

The answer to this doubt would be tantamount to deciding whether the Teilhardian vision of the universe and its "spiritualistic evolutionism" is proven or at least likely. We believe that in its essentials it more than holds its own with materialistic theories and that its solidity does not depend on the ultimate prolongations of the system. We will simply note here that this second kind of optimism reproduces exactly—and no more—the "optimism" of the entire tradition of spiritualistic philosophy which in other ways affirms the immortality of the human soul.

Just as St. Augustine, St. Thomas, or Descartes profess that the soul is immortal, so Teilhard professes that the progress of the cosmos, giving birth to beings endowed with a spiritual and personal soul, is an irreversible progress. Its context is no longer individual and static, it is collective and dynamic, but on either side the final affirmation is the same.[116] Through the medium of his "phenomenology" he wishes to apply the same answer "to the ancient problem (so parascientific in appearance) of immortality," [117] and the "energetic" way adopted most often by him in his argumentation is very close to the Thomistic argumentation of the "desiderium naturale" ["natural desire"] which one commentary recently characterized as constituting "an apodictic demonstration." [118]

Only, in a more concrete perspective which more directly recalls that of Christian Revelation, he endeavors to show how in "a unique and supreme event, . . . the Historical must be welded to the Transcendent." "An opening exists," an "outlet"; Thought will never be snuffed out, "still-born in a self-abortive and absurd universe"; in the future we have waiting for us "not only continuation but also *survival*": such is for Teilhard the conviction that gives the basis for an "absolute optimism." [119] And it is through this that he wished "to give hope to man's work and inquiry." [120] "To know that we are not imprisoned. To know that there is an outlet, and air, light, and love, in some measure, on the other side of total death. To know this without delusion or fiction!" [121] In a world "open at its summit *in Christo Jesu* [in Christ Jesus], we are now safe from the threat of suffocation! And instead, there flows down from these heights not only air to breathe but the radiance of love descending upon us." [122]

Option and "Segregation"

However, since the spirit, being reflective consciousness, is essentially freedom[123]—the "rise of interiority" being identically the rise "of freedom"—all this in no way prejudges the final lot of each individual person, that is, the sign whether negative or positive which must mark his decisive consummation. For beginning with man, and through man, "evolution has now to make its own choice";[124] everyone can use this fearsome power of free will either well or badly: the moral and religious choice which Teilhard constantly returns to invoke either apropos of individuals of every age or apropos of the last human generation.

It is even found in contexts in which it would not seem to be indispensable. Thus, we find it at the end of lessons conducted at the Sorbonne on a highly scientific-technical plane, consecrated to *Man's Place in Nature*. After showing that the human species must possess an "Outlet," through which it can at the end of its course escape "total death," Père Teilhard adds, coming back to the present: "Nothing, apparently, can prevent man-the-species from growing still greater (just as man-the-individual —for good . . . or for evil) . . ." [125]

This dramatic alternative is furthermore presented on various occasions as the alternative of the attitude of the Titans and Prometheus, or the attitude of Jacob; the attitude of "revolt," or "adoration"; of "haughty Power" or "evangelical sanctity"; of "arrogant autonomy" or "loving excentration"; of the rejection or the acceptance of Omega. [126] Besides the "ambiguous term" which is the "spirit of the earth," the dilemma is posed by the "spirit of force" which is the "spirit of autonomy and solitude" and the "spirit of love" which is the "spirit of service and of giving." [127]

Père Teilhard sometimes expresses the hope that through the effect of a spiritual progress the whole of humanity will incline more toward the saving choice; but even then he always maintains the necessity for the choice. "The world does not open, for him, like a flower, when it reaches the inevitable term of its history; it is still divided in a kind of ultimate ramification before opening itself to the ardor of Christ." [128] If there is therefore a philosophy for which "evil vanishes like a shadow to the extent that thought proves itself capable of extending its empire forward," this philosophy is not his.

In Teilhardian language there is a key word, with a hierarchy of analogical significations, which serves to demonstrate the agreement of this real alternative, that is, the risk of damnation, with the infallibility of the work of God. Correlative to the word "aggregation" is the word "segregation."

The Teilhardian "segregation" can be compared—provided all quantitative connotation be eliminated—with the biblical ideas of the "Rest" of Israel. We should also note that it is found in all modes as well as all levels of being: there is a geological segregation, [129] a cosmic segregation, a spiritual segregation, and a Christic segregation. In every order as in every degree, "the creative synthesis entails uprootings, each aggregation being accompanied by a segregation."

Cosmic segregation: our universe is composed in some way of two parts, originally united (Teilhard even says at one point: of two universes), which are moving apart and separating. The split takes place right from the roots: on one side there is the "cosmos which segregates itself through life" then through thought; on the other, "the cosmos which is not connected, not informed, and so dies and is dispersed." These have been regarded as what he elsewhere terms the ordered and disordered, or, in dynamic terms, the two great inverted phenomena of convergence and entropy.[130]

The same law is verified analogically in the spiritual life. Père Teilhard establishes, for example, that his instinctive tendency as a believer is "to integrate all things in Christ." But this, he quickly specifies, does not at all signify that he worked "to preserve all things." He realizes that integration, no matter how universal, essentially entails a segregation, that is in this case, in correlative fashion a "renunciation." What he desires and what he strives for is, by a process that could equally be compared to a distillation, "to seize all the *nisus,* all the élan and the power of life in the universe." He wished "no particle of energy to be lost."

Finally, the same is true of the Body of Christ. In an ultimate state, it is humanity (= the cosmos) consummated in God. But this "total Body" (to speak like Origen) is only formed, over the course of centuries and is finally completed only through a rigorous segregation. Even this Père Teilhard wants to make precise. In the course of the year 1916, during the time when his most personal thought was taking root, he noted (on October 7): "In writing 'the world in Christ' I must introduce into evidence simultaneously *the enervation of all* in Christ or through Christ *and* the segregationist character of this organization."

And, indeed, this is fairly well what he did. "The new earth is in formation on all sides. Around the completed center which is the humanity of Christ (and of his mother) the Nebulae is in process of segregation and concentration, its elements being throughout, although still mingled and diffused, separable above all in the future (much more than in the present): the cockle is not yet adequately distinguished from the good wheat. . . ."

The doctrine of Christic segregation is opposed by Père Teilhard to the doctrines which he terms "false segregation" preached by "false Christs": for example, to the myth of the "future humanity" (obviously, not because he disbelieved in a "human future," but because he conceived it in another way and did not make an absolute out of it). This is also what he opposes to "pagan pantheism," which excludes the very idea of segregation and envisages "only fusion with the initial Whole: hence, no true degree in being, no progress, no lateral clusters, and *no waste.*"

Again, thanks to this it is possible for him clearly to distinguish the two truths—related but quite different—which more than one theologian of our day is at pains not to confuse: on the one hand, the assumption of the whole of human nature by the Word of God made flesh which results in an essential and inalienable rapport of all men with Christ, and on the other hand, the constitution of the mystical Body of Christ of which every man is not a member by the mere fact of being a man.[131]

Put another way, if Christ appeared to Teilhard "surrounded with the glory of the world," this signifies for him "glorified by everything that is blessed in reality." [132]

Analyzing the same idea of segregation more closely and from another angle, Père Teilhard found himself led to acknowledge that it implied the following three principal elements:

1) "Initial union with the Whole (and thus at least radical coexistence with it forever);

2) "Tendency to separation, to isolation, to the sacrifice of

several things constituting the Whole, and progressive realization of this isolation.

3) "Finally, a progression—not to individual dispersion—but to more close communion with a new Whole, more reduced yet more purified, more homogeneous, more organized. And these various elements in the fundamental segregation in which the life of the cosmos is involved (like the success of the tree in its seed) are called respectively: love of the world, sacrifice, formation of the Body of Christ." [133]

"The movement which aggregates the universe to Christ is in reality a segregation," and "therein lies a formidable mystery." [134]

With the benefit of these analyses, which did not cease to guide his thought, although the word segregation itself became very rare under his pen,[135] Père Teilhard de Chardin can repeat after St. Paul: "And God will be all in all." [136]

Conclusion

We stated at the outset of this second part that the entire work of Père Teilhard de Chardin could be understood, envisaged under a certain aspect, as an exposition of a proof for the irreversibility of the cosmos, that is, of the immortality of personal souls, in order subsequently to lead men to Christ. In concluding, we can say once again, in possibly more modern language, that this work is a continuous dialogue with one of the most widespread varieties of atheism in the 20th century.

It is a *real* dialogue, undertaken and pursued over the course of several decades with numerous representatives of this atheism, encountered either in the world of scientists or among men formed by the school of an atheistic science. Anyone well acquainted with the life as well as the writings of Père Teilhard could insert at this point a lengthy list of proper names; he could recall a good many concrete circumstances, conversations and veritable debates which were not all without a happy conclusion. We might note in passing that this explains the personal tone often evident in the argumentation. Père Teilhard de Chardin is not a philosopher in an ivory tower; he is a man who speaks to other men.

This dialogue is never a dialogue of complacency or facility. Still less, of concessions or resignation. Père Teilhard approaches his interlocutor with the widest of human sympathy; he places himself at the same starting point and goes along with him. But he has too much respect and love for him to preserve him in his illusions. As for himself, he yields to no relativism whatever. Modest, although zealous in the proposition of his personal views, he does not think less of himself for the right to have his own language, which he strives to explain for the best.

Teilhard does not suffer any inferiority complex with respect to his convictions. He does not diminish his faith in Christ for the possession of some "value," which a spirit of poverty would induce him to give up in order the better to accept within himself the values of others. "Nothing," he was able to say, "has ever caused me to be a poor believer." His dialogue is always— what every serious dialogue on the intellectual plane must at least ultimately be—a dialogue of confrontation. It is a healthy example for us today.

We can observe in Père Teilhard beside eminent merits a certain number of tendencies which, freed by their isolation, could lead to abusive consequences. We can also note a good many deficiencies. In regard to the subject treated herein, several of these deficiencies are connected with the point that the links in the scientific chain unfolded by the argumentation might perhaps not all appear equally solid or possess an equally-proven solidity.

Others concern the fact that Père Teilhard, a man of science and intuition, was often very little concerned with formal aspects of philosophical knowledge. His thought is not customarily "critical and reflective." [137] Apropos of this aspect of his expositions, Père Maurice Corvez justly speaks of philosophically "naive" proof, and his philosophy is in effect "naive," a little like the painting of Rousseau, the custom house official. (This does not mean at all that he was himself naive, nor even that he was unaware of certain problems but only that he did not treat them *ex professo*.)

But when a "naive" philosophy is that of a man who is "a unique blend of personal revelation and scientific experience," [138] it has chances of containing a more forceful truth and of acting more efficaciously on the progress of thought than a good many more ambitious philosophies.[139] And the earnestness applied by Père Teilhard de Chardin to his confrontation with atheistic materialism confers on his work an importance which will never be possessed by a good many apparently more subtle works. That is why nowadays many feel they should take it seriously.

APPENDICES
AND NOTES

Short Sketch of Teilhard's Life

Pierre Teilhard de Chardin was born on May 1, 1881 in Sarcenat, France, into a devout and land-holding family. As a boy he was already intensely interested in the stones and rocks found on his family's land and the surrounding regions.

He attended high school at the College of Mongré, where he was taught by Henri Bremond, and completed his college course there as well.

On March 20, 1899 Teilhard entered the Jesuit novitiate in Aixen-Provence. He studied philosophy on the island of Jersey (1902–1905), taught college chemistry and physics as a scholastic in Cairo (1905–1908) and pursued his theological studies in Hastings, England (1908–1912). Each of these regions served him well in fostering his interests in geology and paleontology. They also afforded him the opportunity to set his thought down in numerous letters to his friends and loved ones.

Among Teilhard's fellow-scholastics in theology were such men as Pierre Rousselot (who made his reputation with a brilliant work on the "Intellectualism of St. Thomas Aquinas" before incurring a premature death in World War I), Joseph Huby (who went on to become a world-renowned Scripture scholar), Auguste Valensin (his life-long friend and confidant, and a theologian in his own right), and Pierre Charles (another world-famous theologian and author of the best-selling *Prayers for All Times*).

Yet it is clear that Teilhard was up to their level even in theology. For example, he was chosen three years running to defend the classic theses in the formal "disputations."

After his ordination on August 24, 1911, the young priest was sent to Paris for further study in geology (1912–1914). However, in 1914 he was called up for military service and found himself at the front as a stretcher-bearer for a regiment of Moroccan infantry. His war experiences brought him face to face with the ultimate realities of life and he acquitted himself so well that he was awarded the "Croix de Guerre," "Medaille militaire" and the "Medal of Honor."

All the while, Teilhard continued to write—his thesis on geology, letters to his cousin Marguerite Teillard de Chambon (collected in *The Making of a Mind*) and religious and philosophical essays (*Ecrits de temps du guerre—Writings in Time of War*).

After the war he resumed his studies, received his doctorate in 1922 and from 1920–1923 he held a chair in geology at the *Institut Catholique* in Paris. He conducted field trips to China and continued to write.

In 1925 Teilhard was denounced and had to resign his professorship because some of his writings (displayed without his consent) had created some disquiet. The real reason seemed to be because of his open acceptance of evolution.

He left for China in 1925 and worked out of Peking till the end of World War II. He visited France occasionally and lectured in Somalia, Burma, the Indies, Java and the United States.

During these years Teilhard became one of the great specialists of East Asian geology and paleontology. He also played a leading role as an expert in the Chu-Ku-Tien when the first skull of *Homo Sinanthropus* was discovered in 1929, and in its interpretation.

All the while his energetic mind continued to compose various letters, a number of essays intended for his close associates and friends, and articles for reviews. The winter of 1926–1927 saw the birth of *The Divine Milieu* a synthesis of his spiritual experiences of the preceding twelve years. Unfortunately, word leaked out about Pierre Charles' intention to include this work in the *Museum Lessianum* published by the Jesuits of Louvain and authorities in Rome stopped publication.

From 1938 to 1940 Teilhard wrote *The Phenomenon of Man,* his major work (which was to establish his reputation even more when finally published). Unfortunately, it too was prevented from publication till after his death. This work is penetrated and sustained by scientific evolutionism. Starting from the data of his own science, Teilhard develops a vision of the world and of man designed to be acceptable to any impartial observer, whether Christian or not. It bridges the span of evolution from the distant past to the future development of mankind—but with an explicitly Christian bias.

All during the course of World War II Teilhard was in Peking, pursuing his work and doing a limited amount of lecturing. In

May, 1946 he returned to Paris and began giving lectures once again.

Teilhard returned to the United States in 1948 and was able to expound his ideas in scientific circles and before a wider audience, propounding his ideal of a new anthropology that could include man as a spiritual being in its subject matter.

In October, 1948 Teilhard journeyed to Rome hoping to obtain a twofold authorization: (1) to accept a chair of paleontology at the *Collège de France* which had been offered him as a sign of his status in the French world of science and thought; and (2) to publish his *Phenomenon of Man* which had been undergoing revision for more than five years already. He received a heartbreaking refusal to both requests.

From then on Teilhard wrote various religious and scientific works or essays which could not be published (since 1947 his superiors had asked him not to deal with philosophical and theological problems): *Comment je crois* [*How I Believe*] (1948), *Le Christique* [*The Christic*] (1955), etc.

However, he was allowed to give a series of lectures at the Sorbonne in 1949–1950 which became *Man's Place in Nature*— a sober and balanced synopsis of his global vision of nature. In May, 1950 he was elected a member of the Academy of Sciences.

In 1951, Teilhard became a scientific associate to the Viking Fund (later the Wenner Gren Foundation) for the support and encouragement of anthropological studies. He remained such till his death, operating from the U.S.

After a few more field trips and a last journey to France in 1954, he returned to the United States feeling the weight of his years and engrossed with the thought of death: "I am going to Him who is coming."

On March 15, 1955 he told friends of his desire to die on Easter Sunday. He went to confession on Holy Saturday and the morning of Easter, (April 10, 1955) assisted at Mass in St. Patrick's Cathedral. That afternoon at the home of friends Pierre Teilhard de Chardin was stricken with a heart attack and went to meet the Lord he had always sought and served in his life and works.

Short Glossary of Teilhard's Vocabulary

Aggregation—Accumulation, by inertia of corpuscles and bodies which do not constitute an organic whole. The opposite of complexity.

Amorization—The process of mutual attraction of elements in the universe in terms of the conception of energy proper to Teilhard. The cosmos is essentially a force of love tending toward the absolute and personal.

Anthropogenesis—Evolutionary birth of the human species triggered by the mutation of hominization that leads to reflective consciousness.

Anthropology—The science of man, or mankind, in the widest sense—by means of the natural, social, cultural, moral, philosophical, and theological sciences.

Arrangement (or ordering)—The evolutionary tendency of elements of matter to be arranged or ordered into ever more complex structures and organisms finally culminating in man —the most complex.

Biogenesis—Evolutionary formation of life and the phenomena contributing to it. It follows cosmogenesis and precedes psychogenesis.

Biology—The science of life, dealing with organized beings, or animals, or plants.

Biosphere—The actual skin of organic substance which we see today enveloping the earth; a truly structural layer of the planet. Above this lies the noosphere.

Centration (Centreity)—The evolutionary process whereby the "within" of things (their immanence) grows in living and then thinking beings in proportion to the complexification of the "without." Similarly, individual consciousnesses combine to form collective consciousness. There is a supreme center of centration which influences all phenomena—the Omega point or God.

Christ—Can be looked at from various aspects:

Cosmic Christ—The superior psycho-biological focus on whom the universe is completely dependent.

Evolutive Christ—The supreme Mover of cosmogenesis who is forever acting within evolution.

Historical Christ—The historical figure who was born of Mary, went about doing good, suffered and died on the cross.

Mystic(al) Christ—The Consolidator of the whole human genus in the unity of his church.

Omega Christ—Universal Center and Ultimate Point of convergence of cosmic evolution.

Total Christ—Christ together with all who are centered in him in one body (Mystical Body of Christ). The Pauline Christ.

Universal Christ—The center of radiation for the energies which lead the universe back to God through his humanity; "physical influence" of Christ on all things. Synonymous with the Incarnation.

Christic—The union of Christ with evolving humanity and his influence over it.

Christic sense—Consciousness of the omnipresence of Christ and of his mystic energy that fills the universe.

Christify—To render humanity Christlike.

Christogenesis—Evolutionary formation of the Total Christ— the Mystical Body united with its Head, Christ. This is simply the extension of noogenesis which is the culmination of cosmogenesis.

Coherence—Everything in the universe has a common origin and works toward a common goal.

Complexity—The quality whereby living forms pursue an ever more complicated structurization beginning from simple molds and terminating in interiorization. Opposite of Aggregation.

Consciousness—Through successive evolutionary mutations it is: (1) "radial force" or "psychism" in inert matter; (2) simple consciousness of *perception* in animals; (3) *reflective* consciousness in man.

Convergence—Synthetic movement toward an ultimate focus or meeting-point followed by the whole of evolving creation.

After an initial stage of *dispersion* or *divergence,* convergence appears as an *aggregation* in elements and *socialization* in man. Even in the realm of intellectual disciplines (including religion) convergence occurs, since they all approach the same reality.

Cosmic—Pertaining to the cosmos.

Cosmic sense—Perception through the multiple of the basic unity of the universe.

Cosmogenesis—Evolutionary formation of the cosmos in space and time and the evolutive phenomena involved. Modern conception of the universe.

Cosmos—The structured whole of the material, vegetable, animal, and human world.

Derivative—The irresistible movement through which things evolve by the very process of evolution; the directions taken by thought in the evolutionary process yielding the psyche.

Divergence—Opposite of convergence.

Emergence—Appearance of new unforeseeable properties in the process of synthesizing evolution.

Energy—The measure of that which passes from one atom to another in the course of their transformations—a unifying power and the expression of structure. The most primitive form of universal stuff.

Entropy—The name given in physics to the apparently inevitable fact by which series of corpuscles (the seat of all physico-chemical phenomena) slide, by virtue of statistical laws of probability, toward an intermediate state of diffuse agitation; a state in which all exchange of useful energy ceases on our scale of experience. It is the decline or diminution of utilizable energy.

Epiphenomenon (also *paraphenomenon*)—A phenomenon joined to the principal phenomenon without changing either the significance or the evolution of the latter.

Evolution—Theory that all things derive from more simple pre-existing things. For Teilhard this takes place both on the biological and on the psychical plane in accord with his law of complexity-consciousness.

Excentration—Renunciation of one's own center and tendency toward a superior one.

Extrapolation—The means whereby a curve is constructed, with the aid of positive data, beyond what can be observed. Teilhard uses it to preview the future of evolution by reasoning on the unity and coherence of the universe.

Freedom—Power of self-determination whereby man relates himself to various values.

Hominization—The passage of evolution from the state of non-reflective living animal to the human or reflective state.

Immanent—That which exists and acts in the very center of things, and is in accord with their natural responsibilities.

Immortality—The end of a reflective species—not a disaggregation and death, but a new opening and a rebirth (outside time and space) through an excess of unification and co-reflection.

Integration—Unification of diverse parts of a whole constituting a new unity.

Interiorization—Development of psychism or consciousness in things.

Interiority—Synonym for consciousness.

Law of complexity-consciousness—Left long enough to itself, under the prolonged and universal play of chance, matter manifests the property of arranging itself in more and more complex groupings, and at the same time in ever-deepening layers of consciousness; this double and combined movement of physical unfolding and psychic interiorization (or centration) once started, continuing, accelerating and growing to its utmost extent.

Law of Recurrence—Every law according to which the same property in a series is reencountered on different levels, intervals and times, allowing for higher synthesis.

Matter—Used in three senses: (a) *ordinary sense*—what appears to our senses; (b) *metaphysical sense*—determinable principle in opposition to the determining principle, *form;* (c) *physical sense*—primordial form of the stuff of the universe, composed of the "within" and the "without."

Monad—Every element considered as bearer of a psychism centered on itself independently of synthesis in which it can enter; a micro-universe.

Movement—It is continuous and inherent in things, following the law of complexity-consciousness, and providing the basis of evolution.

Multiple—The first condition of the stuff of the universe was extreme multiplicity, which is slowly unified by evolution.

Mutation—Sudden modification introduced into the descendence of a living species, signalling the birth of a new biological orientation.

Mystique—State of one who lives the unity of all things at the level of the spirit.

Noogenesis—Genesis of reflective thought which follows the genesis of non-reflective consciousness or *psychogenesis*.

Noosphere—The human thinking "skin" which covers the earth; the energetic envelope formed by the entire spiritual activity of men.

Omega—Point of convergence toward which the whole of evolution and humanity is progressing. Center of attraction and ultimate point of concentration of the reflective psychism of the noosphere. In the final analysis this is God, Center of centers and more specifically *Christ*.

Orthogenesis—A line of continuous evolutionary progress obtained by micromutations, always in the same sense either on the biological or on the psychical plane. Biological term for the law of controlled complication; used to single out the manifest property of living matter to form a system in which terms succeed each other experimentally, following the constantly increasing degrees of centro-complexity.

Parousia—The fulfillment of evolution at the end of time corresponding to the Second Coming of Christ.

Person—Conscious being, with reflective thought.

Personalist—View that sees man as possessing a proper, original and immortal value.

Personalization—An internal deepening of consciousness on itself. Collectively, it is a union that exercises an enriching effect on individual and collective consciousness.

Phenomenon—Taken in its primordial meaning it includes everything presenting itself as an objective datum to human cognition and experience. It constitutes part of the "hyper-physics" or "hyper-biology" which makes up Teilhard's phenomenology.

Phenomenology—A scientific method for arriving at the knowledge of observable phenomena. Teilhard includes manifestations of consciousness in the latter which are usually reserved for philosophy.

Phylum—Branch of the genealogical tree of the living.

Pleroma—Plenitude. The constitution of the Mystical Body of Christ which corresponds to the created multiple, the personal consciousnesses.

Psychogenesis—See *Noogenesis*.

Psychism—See *Consciousness*.

Reflection—Ability of man's consciousness to look at itself and evaluate his thought and action.

Space-Time—Einsteinian notion regarding this as a *continuum*. Teilhard does not "spacialize" time.

Spirit and Matter—Distinct, but like two faces of one same energy. The spirit of man possesses a constitution that enables it to subsist after being detached from matter.

Spirit of the Earth—Ensemble of human consciousness.

Stuff of the Universe—Initial energy—still undifferentiated—from which the world is made, possessing a "within" and a "without," a material and a spiritual aspect.

Survival—Life apart from time and space.

Synthesis—Arrangement of elements over the course of evolution in ever-more complex unities, ultimately terminating in Christ, source of all synthesis.

Transcendent—The fact of surpassing something either *relatively* (life transcends matter but stems from it) or *absolutely* (God transcends creation but does not come from it).

Transformism—Theory concerning the origin and evolution of beings.

Ultra-human—Future state of humanity when the collective consciousness and unanimization will be established. Its union with Omega at the end of time will usher in the trans-human state.

Ultra-personal—Corresponds to the statute of a personal God.

Ultra-physics—A science that is not yet elaborated which seeks to elucidate the phenomena in their physico-psychic intricateness and evolve a coherent explanation of the universe.

Unanimization—Realization of a planetary humanity united in a common effort to promote spiritual progress.

Vortex—Metaphorical designation of the turbulence of the universe which concentrically uncoils itself on itself.

List of Teilhard's Works Cited in This Book

> (*Works already translated are given only in English; the abbreviation in parentheses refers to the volume—English or French—of Teilhard's collected works in which each appears; the key to the abbreviation is indicated at the end of this list—an asterisk indicates an unpublished work.*)

1916   La Vie Cosmique (ETG)—The Cosmic Life
       La Maîtrise du Monde et le règne de Dieu (ETG)— Mastery of the World and the Kingdom of God
       Christ in the World of Matter (HU; ETG)
1917   La Lutte contre la multitude (ETG)—The Struggle against the Multitude
       Le Milieu mystique*—The Mystic Milieu
       L'Union créatrice (ETG)—The Creative Union
1918   L'Ame du Monde (ETG)—The Soul of the World
       La Grande Monad (ETG)—The Grand Monad
       Le Prêtre (ETG)—The Priest
       La Foi qui opère (ETG)—The Faith That Works
       Forma Christi (ETG)—The Form of Christ
1919   Note pour servir a l'évangélisation des temps nouveaux (ETG)—Note Intended for the Evangelization of New Times
       Les Noms de la matière (ETG)—The Names of Matter
1920   Note sur le Christ universel (SC)—Note on the Universal Christ
1921   Science et Christ, ou Analyse et Synthèse (SC)—Science and Christ, or Analysis and Synthesis
1923   The Mass on the World (HU)
1924   Mon Univers (SC)—My Universe
1926   The Basis and Foundations of the Idea of Evolution (VP)
1926–
1927   The Divine Milieu (DM)
1929   Le Sens humain*—The Human Sense

1930 What Should We Think of Transformism? (VP)
1931 L'Esprit de la terre (EH)—The Spirit of the Earth
1933 Le Christianisme dans le monde (SC)—Christianity in the World
1934 Comment je crois*—How I Believe
1936 Esquisse d'un Univers personel (AE)——Sketch of a Personal Universe

   Quelques réflexions sur la conversion du monde (SC)—Some Reflections on the Conversion of the World
1937 Le Phenomène spirituel (EH)—The Spiritual Phenomenon

   L'Energie humain (EH)—Human Energy
1938–
1940 The Phenomenon of Man (PM)
1939 La Mystique de la Science (EH)—The Mystique of Science

   The Grand Option (FM)
1940 La Parole attendue (CA-4)—The Long-Awaited Word
1941 The Future of Man Seen by a Paleontologist (FM)

   L'Atomisme de l'Esprit (AE)—The Atomism of the Spirit
1942 The 'Conic' Transposition of Action (The New Spirit) (FM)

   Le Christ evoluteur*—The Evolutive Christ

   Man's Place in the Universe: Reflections on Complexity (VP)
1943 Super-humanité, super-Christ, super-Charité (SC)—Super-Humanity, Super-Christ, Super-Charity

   Réflexions sur le bonheur (CA-2)—Reflections on Happiness
1944 La Centrologie (AE)—Centrology
1945 Action et Activation (SC)—Action and Activation

   Life and the Planets (FM)

   Christianisme et Evolution*—Christianity and Evolution
1946 Some Reflections on the Spiritual Repercussions of the Atom Bomb (FM)

   Esquisse d'un dialectique de l'esprit (AE)—Sketch of a Dialectic of the Spirit
1947 Place de la technique dans un biologie générale de l'humanité (AE)—The Place of Technology in a General Biology of Mankind
1948 The Directions and Conditions of the Future (FM)

   Trois choses que je vois*—Three Things That I See

Collections (and Abbreviations) of Teilhard's Works

CA-1,   Cahiers Pierre Teilhard de Chardin—Notebooks: Pierre
2,3,4,5   Teilhard de Chardin (Vols. 1–5)

Collections of Letters

1914–1919	The Making of a Mind
1919	Correspondence (with M. Blondel)
1917–1934	Letters to Père Auguste Valensin
1923–1955	Letters from a Traveller
	Textes et Documents Inédits (à Léontine Zanta) —Unpublished Texts and Documents (to Léontine Zanta)

NOTES

Translator's Note

1. Part of a reply to a question concerning Teilhard that followed Rahner's lecture on "The Task of Theology after the Council" found in John H. Miller, C.S.C. (ed.) *Vatican II: An Interfaith Appraisal* (Notre Dame-London: University of Notre Dame Press, 1966), p. 603.
2. *Ibid.*

Part One

1. Allocution of April 23, 1955, in Henri de Lubac, *The Religion of Teilhard de Chardin* (New York: Desclée Co., 1967), pp. 268–271. Cf. R. d'Ouince, L'Epreuve de l'obéissance dans la vie du Père Teilhard in the collective work: *L'Homme devant Dieu* (Paris: Aubier, Coll. "Théologie," 1964), vol. 3, pp. 340–341.
2. *Le Prêtre* (1918), 4: l'Apostolat (*Ecrits du temps de la guerre,* Paris: B. Grasset, 1965, p. 297).
3. *Ecrits . . . ,* p. 307. Cf. Matt. 14, 28–31.
4. *L'Union créatrice (Ecrits . . . ,* pp. 191–192). *The Divine Milieu* (New York: Harper & Row, 1965), p. 136. Letter to Marguerite Teilhard-Chambon, August 28, 1918 (*The Making of a Mind,* New York: Harper & Row, Publishers, 1961, p. 231). Letter to P. Auguste Valensin, December 17, 1922: "We must ever go forward courageously and filially. The waters will carry us onward if we are going toward the Lord." Letter to L. Zanta, August 22, 1928 (*Lettres à Lèontine Zanta,* Paris: Desclée de Brouwer, coll. "Christus," 1965, p. 89). Retreats of 1948. Cf. Henri de Lubac, *Teilhard de Chardin: The Man and His Meaning* (New York: The New American Library, 1967, A Mentor-Omega Book), pp. 76, 84, 85, 150.
5. Letter to M. Teillard-Chambon, June 29, 1916 (*The Making of a Mind,* p. 107).
6. Cf. *The Religion . . . ,* pp. 228–229.
7. Cf. *Teilhard de Chardin . . . ,* pp. 174–183.
8. *La Vie Cosmique* (1916) (*Ecrits . . . ,* p. 42). Letters to M. Teillard-Chambon, October 4, 1917 and September 17, 1919 (*The Making of a Mind,* pp. 206 and 307–308); to L. Zanta, October 15, 1926 (*op. cit.,* p. 79); to Auguste Valensin, June 21, 1921.

9. Allocution to the Pontifical Academy of Sciences, October 13, 1963.

10. Letter to Auguste Valensin, June 21, 1921: "At least may our desires be the dust from which such a man will emerge!" To the same person on December 31, 1926: "Oh! how much I would have liked to have met the St. Ignatius or St. Francis of Assisi that our age so sadly needs! What a wonderful dream—to follow a man of God along a free, fresh road, impelled by the full force of the religious life-sap *of his own time!* Often I pray to God that I may be the ashes from which will arise, for other generations, the great blaze that our own looks for in vain" (cited in *The Religion* . . . , p. 20). Cf. the desire of Abbé Monchanin: "I would so like to be the precursor of the saint who will convert India . . ." (cited by Edouard Duperray, "Vers la communion trinitaire" in *Spiritus,* 26 [1965], p. 55). See also Jules Monchanin, *Ecrits spirituels,* assembled by Edouard Duperray (Paris: Ed. du Centurion, 1965).

11. *Christ in the World of Matter* (1916), I, The Picture (*Hymn of the Universe,* New York and Evanston: Harper & Row, publishers, 1965, p. 45).

12. Origen, "Sur l'Epître aux Ephésiens," fragment 8, 7–10 in *The Journal of Theological Studies,* 3, p. 242.

13. Etienne Gilson, in *Seminarium,* 1965, p. 223.

14. *Le Milieu mystique* (1917). *Forma Christi, note sur l'Elément universel* (1918). *Le Christique* (1955), etc. Cf. *Teilhard de Chardin* . . . , pp. V–VII.

15. Letter of January 7, 1934. Already on August 28, 1926, to Léontine Zanta: "I am particularly struck at this moment by the period of waiting and expectation in which humanity finds itself with respect to its most essential need which is that of a faith" (*Op. cit.,* p. 76). He readily divided his writings into two categories: "ad usum Christianorum" [for the use of Christians] and "ad usum gentilium" [for the use of Gentiles].

16. Concerning the friendship of Père Charles and Teilhard, see Pierre Teilhard de Chardin and Maurice Blondel, *Correspondence,* with notes and commentary by Henri de Lubac, introduction (New York: Herder and Herder, 1967).

17. Letter of January 7, 1934, etc.

18. Letter to Léontine Zanta, April 3, 1930: "I have been requested— and would like—to write a kind of exposition of Christianity for the use of the youth of China. It will be entitled: "The Place of Christianity in the Universe" (*Op. cit.,* p. 114).

19. Letter of June 19, 1926 (*Letters from a Traveller,* New York: Harper & Brothers Publishers, 1962, p. 128).

20. Letter of June 21, 1921.

21. *Quelques réflexions sur la conversion du monde* (1936) (*Œuvres,* Paris: Ed. du Seuil, vol. 9, p. 157).

22. Cf. Hans Urs von Balthasar, *Dieu et l'homme aujourd'hui* (tr. Robert Givord, Paris: Desclée de Brouwer, 1958), p. 102: "By the simultaneous appearance of the world of technology and the history of nature, a revo-

lution has taken place in the order of world-vision; at present man dominates nature, from which he has elevated himself as a being of nature."

23. *Réflexions sur la probabilité scientifique et les conséquences religieuses d'un ultra-humain,* Easter 1951 (*Œuvres,* vol. 7, p. 289).

24. Letter of January 7, 1934. Cf. *Christologie et Evolution* (1935): "By dint of abstractly repeating and developing the expression of our dogmas, we are on the way to getting lost in the clouds which are no longer penetrated either by the affairs, the aspirations or the vigor of earth." *The Heart of the Problem* (1949): "Christianity will lose, to the extent that it fails to embrace . . . *everything that is human on earth,* the keen edge of its vitality and its full power to attract" (*The Future of Man,* New York and Evanston: Harper & Row, Publishers, 1964, p. 265).

25. *Le Prêtre* (*Ecrits* . . . , pp. 298–299).

26. *Note pour servir à l'évangélisation des temps nouveaux* (*Ecrits* . . . , p. 380). It is further fitting to note that in this work he is dealing only with a preliminary question, with a view to attaining for Jesus Christ the head and the heart of humanity. And those who have stumbled over the formula: "Gospel of human effort" have not read to the very end of the opuscule; they would then have seen that the third period of the program outlined for the spiritual life of the Christian consisted in "sublimating the human effort by enabling him to attain (by the prolongation of himself) superior forms of activity which are purity, contemplation, death in God."

27. An author who is not always a faithful interpreter of the Teilhardian thought has nevertheless justly written: "The fundamental ambition of Père Teilhard de Chardin is to grasp and integrate into Christianity the most vital forces of our age: science and the human construction of the future": R. Garaudy, *Perspectives de l'homme* (*Paris: P.U.F.,* 1961), p. 196. If this does not represent the entire Teilhardian project, it constitutes an essential part of it.

28. Letter of June 21, 1921. Cf. above, Ms. p. 10, note 20.

29. *La Maîtrise du Monde et le Règne de Dieu, Introduction* (*Ecrits* . . . , p. 67). *Trois choses que je vois* (1948). Cf. Hans Urs von Balthasar, "Three Signs of Christianity": "There is only one single 'synthesis' (of God and the world): Christ, the Word of the Father, present in the flesh" in *Théologie de l'Histoire* (Paris: Desclée de Brouwer, 1955), p. 195. (The English version does not contain this part: *A Theology of History,* New York: Sheed & Ward, 1963.)

30. From whom he does not separate St. John. Cf. *Christianisme et Evolution* (Peking, 1935). *The Phenomenon of Man* (New York: Harper & Row, 1955), pp. 296–297. In a report presented to the "Colloquy of Vezelay" (1965) Père Elliot showed the points of agreement which also exist between the Christology of Père Teilhard and that of the Gospel according to St. Mark.

31. *L'Union créatrice* (November, 1917), p. 2 (*Ecrits* . . . , p. 196).

32. *La Pensée du Père Teilhard de Chardin* (Paris: Ed. Seuil, 1964).

33. *Christologie et Evolution* (1933). *Quelques réflexions sur la conversion du monde* (1936).

34. The same is true of all analogous cases. We can ask, for example, without disrespect toward St. Thomas, if the transposition he effected from the Aristotelian contemplation to Christian contemplation found in him its full fruition. Cf. Lucien-Marie de Saint-Joseph, *L'Impatience de Dieu* (1964), p. 268: "Eight of the nine reasons given by him are taken from Aristotle (*Secunda secundae*, q. 182, art. 1). Doubtless, these reasons have been baptized. Doubtless, too, their content is profoundly transformed by recourse to Scripture, etc. Still, there is no less danger in this recourse to a vocabulary taken from a contemplation which is not that of the Gospel. . . ."

35. See the references in *Teilhard de Chardin . . .* , p. 41. This is also the interpretation of Christopher F. Mooney, S.J. "The Body of Christ in the Writings of Teilhard de Chardin" in *Theological Studies* (1964), 25, p. 604. Cf. also a later work: *Teilhard de Chardin and the Mystery of Christ* (New York: Harper & Row, Publishers, 1964), pp. 94 ff.

36. References will be found in *Teilhard de Chardin . . .* , pp. 35–44. See also Theodore of Mopsuestia, *Third Catechetical Homily* no. 9; Athanasius, *On the Incarnation of the Word*, ch. 45. *L'Ame du Monde* (Epiphany, 1918): "Far from eclipsing Christ, the universe finds its stability only in him." (*Ecrits . . .* , pp. 227–228). Concerning Col. 1, 16 consult André Feuillet, "La création de l'univers dans le Christ," in *New Testament Studies*, 12, pp. 1–9. Cf. O. Cullmann, *La foi et le culte de l'Eglise primitive* (1963), pp. 13–15.

37. Cf. Romano Guardini, *Le Seigneur* (Paris-Strasbourg, Alsatia, 1945), I, pp. 250–251. Paul Beauchamp, "Le salut corporel des justes et la conclusion du Livre de la Sagesse," in *Biblica* (1964), p. 496.

38. *The Meaning of Paul for Today* (Cleveland & New York: The World Publishing Co., Meridian Books, 1957), p. 90. Compare this with the "concrete universal" notion of Maurice Blondel, *Exigences philosophiques du Christianisme*, p. 185.

39. *Teilhard de Chardin . . .* , pp. 49–54. Teilhard's formulas on this subject which have been criticized are entirely in conformity with tradition. See, for example, Theophylactius, Commentary on the Epistle to the Ephesians, in reference to chapter 1, 3: "Christ is fulfilled in all his members" (Migne, P.G., 124, 1049–1050 BC: "For Christ will be fulfilled and as if consummated through all his members in all the faithful. . . . For then will our Head Christ be fulfilled, that is, he will receive a perfect body, when all of us will be joined and welded together").

40. *The Divine Milieu*, p. 117.

41. Written in 1919. The ardor of his desire never knew any decline. It might be interesting to note that in 1961 at New Delhi the representatives of the young (Protestant) Afro-Asiatic Churches reproached European Protestantism for having let the cosmic dimension of Christ

become obscured over the centuries: Helmut Riedlinger, "The Universal Kingship of Christ," in *Concilium,* 11 (January, 1966), p. 126, note 35.

42. *Teilhard de Chardin . . . ,* pp. 143–161.

43. Saint-Paul, *Epîtres de la captivité* (Collection "Verbum Salutis," Paris: Beauchesne), p. 40.

44. Concerning St. Paul and Stoicism: J. Dupont, *Gnosis* (Louvain-Paris, 1949), pp. 431–435, etc. See *Teilhard de Chardin . . . ,* pp. 176–178. It was through Léontine Zanta, author of a thesis on Stoicism in the 16th century (*le Stoïcisme au seizième siècle*), that Teilhard had discovered the meaning of Stoic pantheism: letter of April 14, 1919 (*The Making of a Mind,* p. 291).

45. *Note sur le Christ universel* (1920); *Œuvres,* vol. 9, pp. 43–44). *Le sens humain* (1929). *Comment je crois* (1934). *Quelques réflexions sur la conversion du monde* (1936).

46. Letter to Père J. B. Janssens, Cape Town, October 12, 1951 (*Letters from a Traveller,* pp. 42–43).

47. *Nova et vetera* (Fribourg), 1965, p. 306.

48. *La Mystique de la Science* (1939) (*Œuvres,* vol. 6, pp. 220–221).

49. January 1, 1951. It is principally in this perspective that the texts of Père Teilhard on the Eucharist should be regarded (see *Teilhard de Chardin . . . ,* part I, ch. 8, pp. 59–64). Cf. Jean Mouroux. *La Seigneurie de Jésus-Christ:* It is "in a mysterious and sealed sign—the Eucharist—that the transfiguration of the world and human travail is inaugurated," while waiting for "the full, marvelous and definitive reality, in which are transfigured in Jesus Christ 'who fills all things' (Eph. 4, 10) mankind and the entire world." (In the Appendix to *Consolez mon peuple* by Paul Gautier: Paris: Editions du Cerf, 1965, pp. 304–305.)

50. Cf. Piet Smulders, *The Design of Teilhard de Chardin* (Westminster: The Newman Press, 1967), pp. 58–59. After remarking that "evolver" is "the grammatical parallel of creator," the author concludes that the "great merit of Teilhard will probably lie in having grasped the necessity for a renewal and another orientation of the image of creation."

51. Letter to Père Teilhard, 1933; cited by Emile Rideau, *La Pensée du Père Teilhard de Chardin* (Paris: Ed. du Seuil, 1963), p. 400.

52. Letter of December 9, 1933 (*italics added;* cited in *Teilhard de Chardin . . . ,* p. 51, note 19).

53. *Comment je crois* (1934). The italics for the word "preserve" are the author's. *Quelques réflexions . . .* (1936): "Christ grows by remaining what he is, or to put it in a better way, *in order to remain* what he was."

54. John Henry Cardinal Newman, *An Essay on the Development of Christian Doctrine* (New York: Doubleday & Company, Inc., 1960, Image Books), part II, ch. 8, p. 337; ch. 5, section 3: "An eclectic, conservative, assimilating, healing moulding process, a unitive power, is of the essence, . . . of a faithful development" (p. 190).

55. In the collective work *La Mystique et les Mystiques,* edited by André Ravier, S.J. (Paris: Desclée de Brouwer, 1965), p. 887. From the same author, *La rencontre des religions* (Paris: Aubier, 1957), p. 46: "The evolutionary Christocentrism of Teilhard de Chardin in sum only restores to Copernican heliocentrism its true spiritual significance," and it does so "by assuming in the Christian faith an eminently Oriental contemplative dimension."

56. Letter of July 4, 1920 (cited—except for the first sentence—in *The Religion* . . . , p. 105). Concerning the relations between Père Teilhard and Père Auguste Valensin, see: Auguste Valensin, *Textes et documents inédits* (Paris: Aubier, 1961) and: Pierre Teilhard de Chardin and Maurice Blondel *Correspondence,* Introduction.

57. Letters of December 17, 1922 and March 23, 1930.

58. See René d'Ouince, S.J., L'épreuve de l'obéissance dans la vie du Père Teilhard de Chardin in *l'Homme devant Dieu,* vol. 3, pp. 334–337. (The citation that follows—from a letter of December 31, 1926—is found in *The Religion* . . . , p. 228.)

59. February 27, 1927 (cited in *The Religion* . . . , p. 364, note 54). Cf. Letter to Léontine Zanta, August 23, 1929: "Everything depends on the evolution of my *official* relations with Rome; and I am very much afraid that I will never succeed in restoring my 'virginity' on this level. I have underlined *official* because as far as the *interior* and profound level is concerned it seems to me that you can rest easy on my part" (*Op. cit.,* pp. 103–104).

60. Père André Ravier alluded to this in the homily given at Paris on March 25, 1965, on the tenth anniversary of Teilhard's death: in the appendix to Pierre Teilhard de Chardin and Maurice Blondel *Correspondence.* In 1934 there was for a moment "vague question" of an invitation from Rome; but the invitation never came and Père Teilhard was counseled against making the trip by his Provincial, Père Christophe de Bonneville. Cf. Letter to Léontine Zanta, June 24, 1934 (*Op. cit.,* p. 123).

61. Conference of Peking, February 22, 1941, on *The Future of Man Viewed by a Paleontologist* (*The Future of Man,* p. 76).

62. Letter to the Very Rev. Msgr. J. Janssens, Cape-Town, October 12, 1951. Cited in Pierre Leroy, *Pierre Teilhard de Chardin tel que je l'ai connu* (Paris: Plon, 1958), p. 57. (English translation found in the article by Leroy—"The Man"—in *Letters from a Traveller,* p. 42.)

63. *Le Phénomène Chrétien.*

64. *Comment je vois* (1948), no. 24 (cited in *The Design of Teilhard de Chardin,* pp. 239–240). Note of October 24, 1921. Cf. *The Phenomenon of Man,* pp. 291–298. *Is There in the Universe a Main Axis of Evolution?*: "The Church is neither an epi- nor a para-phenomenon in the growth of the human social organism, but the very axis (or nucleus) about which it forms" (*Turmoil or Genesis?* in *The Future of Man,* p. 223).

65. Père Loew, O.P., conference given at Saint-Louis-des-Français, Rome,

on October 21, 1965: "Let us unburden our faith from its excess baggage: Too many things weigh us down. The mystery of faith is as it were overcome by casuistry. People are drowning. . . . We must rediscover the major axes of Faith . . . , render the primordial truths dazzling."

66. Cf. His Holiness Paul VI, allocution to his compatriots of Brescia: "How can we combine the riches received from antiquity with those of the recent past and produce new forms? For it is undeniable that our society is in the process of radical change: thought, culture, customs, economy, social life and likewise religious sentiment and its expressions are evolving. How are we to treat the heritage of yesterday in respect to today and tomorrow?"

67. *Christianisme et Evolution. Le Christianisme dans le Monde* (1933) (*Œuvres*, vol. 9, p. 145).

68. *Le Christ évoluteur* (1942). *The Phenomenon of Man*, p. 270: "If by its very nature it did not escape from the time and space which it gathers together, it would not be Omega."

69. Letter to Père A.-D. Sertillanges, February 4, 1934.

70. *Le Christianisme dans le Monde* (May 1932) (*Œuvres*, vol. 9, p. 143; cited in *Teilhard de Chardin . . . , p. 39*).

71. Letter to Père André Ravier, New York, January 14, 1955 (cited in *Teilhard de Chardin . . . , pp. 47–48*). See notes 52 and 53, above.

72. *Christologie et Evolution* (1933) (cited in *Teilhard de Chardin . . . , p. 48*).

73. *Ecrits . . . , p. 279.*

74. Letter of February 16, 1955. Cf. January 14: "It seems to me that we are living again, at a distance of fifteen hundred years, the great battles of Arianism: but with this difference, that the problem today is not to define the relations between the Christic and the Trinitary—but between Christ and a universe that has suddenly become fantastically big, formidably organic, and more than probably poly-human . . ." (cited in *Teilhard de Chardin . . . , p. 47*)! It has recently been written that "a single planet holds Teilhard's attention; it is the land of men. Hence, he is in accord with the philosophers who ignore the cosmic. . . ." In reality, he raises the possibility of other "living planets" not only in *Comment je vois,* but also in *La Centrologie* (*Œuvres*, vol. 7, pp. 133–134). Throughout, his cosmos is really the cosmos and not the earth alone. In a brief study published on this subject in *l'Almanach des sciences* of 1951, he explained why he retraces the history of life on the earth and not elsewhere (*from the Pre-Human to the Ultra-Human: The Phases of a Living Planet* in *The Future of Man*, pp. 289–297). The reason appears obvious.

75. On September 7, 1953, writing from Johannesburg to his Provincial, Père André Ravier, he ascertained with joy in certain milieu "the simultaneous growth of the twofold instinct (or, if you will, the twofold flame) which Christianity so greatly needs at this moment: *sentire [to think]* at the same time and with the same intensity, *cum Mundo et cum*

Ecclesia [*with the World and with the Church*]—and you will understand
in what sense I take "World": the enormous cosmic process of arrangement whose appearance, for anyone who can see, revolutionizes the
totality of our understanding."

76. *La Parole attendue* (Peking, October 31, 1940); *Cahiers Pierre Teilhard de Chardin* (Paris: Editions du Seuil), vol. 4, p. 27. As an aid to
the understanding of this idea of the universal Christ, one can consult
Hans Urs von Balthasar, "Trois Signes de Christianisme" in *Théologie
de l'Histoire*, pp. 180–187 (omitted from English edition). See also
Maurice Blondel, *Exigences philosophiques du Christianisme* (Paris:
Presses Universitaires, 1950), p. 185.

77. *Science et Christ, ou Analyse et synthèse* (1921) (*Œuvres*, vol. 9,
p. 60).

78. *Le Christianisme dans le Monde* (1933) (*Œuvres*, vol. 9, p. 139).

79. Letter of September 6, 1953 (*Letters from a Traveller*, p. 344).
These texts, from very diverse dates, show in this regard the perfect
continuity of his thought even down to the images and formulas it
utilizes. Cf. Péguy, *Clio* 1, p. 281: "The old stock will flourish again, the
old stock will bear fruit," etc.

80. This is what he was already writing on February 7, 1930, saying
that "he was drawn toward 'What is coming,'" but at the same time
assured that this "New thing can only be born from the fidelity to *what
is*": To Léontine Zanta (*Op. cit.*, p. 111). And in 1933: "The times are
ripe for a renewal."

81. This is an allusion to the Encyclical *Humani generis* which his correspondent had used as a pretext for his starting point.

82. October 4, 1950; in Maxime Gorce, *Le Concile et Teilhard* (Neuchâtel, Switzerland, 1963), pp. 196–198. (Cited in part—beginning with the
word "only" excepting the phrase "Neither is this pure speculation"—in
Teilhard de Chardin . . . , p. 180. Cf. a letter to Abbé Breuil, New
York, January 22, 1952: "I remain perfectly calm and optimistic on that
side" (on the future of Christian thought). Cf. letters of July 13, 1925:
"I remain more and more convinced that faith is no longer possible for
the individual, or conversion for peoples, except in a Christianity which
(instead of transforming itself into a force of immobility and reaction
as at present) will be moved to show *by acts* that nothing human can
be achieved without it."

83. With lynx-like eyes our critic perceives this duplicity very early.
Henri Bremond, who taught the humanities to the young Pierre Teilhard
at the college of Mongré has written of him: "Very intelligent, at the
head of his class, but possessed of a despairing sagacity. . . . He had
a jealous and absorbing passion—stones—which caused him to live removed from us." Our critic's commentary: "First testimony that we have
of that essential duplicity of Teilhard." It makes a person want to laugh.

84. Never has Christ "been found lacking" in "his limitless capacity to
fit in with the whole physical and psychological order of our universe":

Le Christianisme dans le Monde (1933), vol. 9, p. 143 (cited in *Teilhard de Chardin . . . ,* p. 39).

85. *Le Concile et Teilhard,* p. 41, etc.; cf. pp. 195–198.

86. *Monogénisme et Monophylétisme.* (On the background of the question see Piet Smulders, *The Design of Teilhard de Chardin,* pp. 188–195.) Cf. the recent *Constitution on the Church (Lumen Gentium),* ch. 4, no. 37: "The laity . . . are, by reason of the knowledge, competence or outstanding ability they may enjoy, permitted and sometimes even obliged to express their opinion on those things that concern the good of the Church." (This was certainly the case with Pierre Teilhard although he was not a layman.) "Let it always be done in truth, in courage and in prudence, with reverence and charity toward those who by reason of their sacred office represent the person of Christ." (Again, this was certainly the case with Teilhard.)

87. *Dynamique du provisoire* (Les Presses de Taizé, 1965), p. 97. In 1953 (June 7), Père Teilhard was to express the hope for a commission to be set up in Rome charged with gathering and examining the reports that might be sent in by men of the various specialties such as himself.

88. *Christologie et Evolution* (1935).

89. René d'Ouince, allocution cited on ms. p. 6, note 1. Cf. letter to Marguerite Teillard, March 7, 1940: "I hope that the Lord will help me, since it is entirely as an attempt to make His countenance seen and loved that I am taking such pains"; *The Making of a Mind,* p. 261. One is reminded of the warning of the *Second Epistle of Peter* concerning the "things difficult to understand, which the unlearned and the unstable distort" (3, 16). Cf. St. Irenaeus, *Adversus Haereses,* I, ch. 41, no. 4.

90. "Le cas Teilhard de Chardin," in *Seminarium,* 17 (1965), pp. 727–728 (part of above text: "harbors . . . writings," cited in P. Chardin and M. Blondel, *Correspondence,* p. 141). We would have only a little more confidence than Mr. Gilson in the echo that the spiritual experience of one person may sometimes find in the conscienciousness of other persons.

91. The passage cited is given in *The Religion . . . ,* p. 17, and identified as belonging to a letter of Oct. 20, 1924. The appeal for translation of Teilhard's thought is from a letter of July 13, 1925, etc. However, we must realize that in his last years especially, he had the tendency to shut himself in his own formulas, too simple for the reality they wished to express, and he sometimes had occasion to misunderstand why they were not adopted as they stood.

92. Claude Cuénot, "Situation de Teilhard de Chardin" in *Tendances* (October, 1962), p. 593.

93. Cf. *Comment je vois* (1948), no. 37.

94. *La Maîtrise du Monde et le Règne de Dieu (Ecrits . . . ,* p. 67; cited in *Teilhard de Chardin . . . ,* p. 170). Letter to Léontine Zanta (*op. cit.,* p. 108), etc. Neither did he ever cease seeking to reunite them and to show their "coherence." Cf. *"The Aims and Scope of the Work of Teilhard de Chardin"* in P. Teilhard and M. Blondel *Correspondence,* pp. 123–135.

95. November 4, 1916 and October 7, 1948. (The latter is found in *Letters from a Traveller*, p. 299.)

96. Letter to Léontine Zanta, May 7, 1927 (*Op. cit.*, p. 87). Cf. P. Teilhard and M. Blondel *Correspondence*, p. 62.

97. *Christianisme et Evolution* (November, 1935).

98. *The Heart of the Problem* (1949): "At the same time Faith in God, in the same degree in which it assimilates and sublimates within its own spirit the spirit of Faith in the world, regains all its power to attract and convert!" (*The Future of Man*, p. 268.) Cf. *The Basis and Foundations of the Idea of Evolution* in *The Vision of the Past* (New York and Evanston: Harper & Row, Publishers, 1966), p. 141. *The Making of a Mind*, p. 307: "The universal, transforming Christ," etc. *Quelques réflexions sur la conversion du monde* (1936): Christianity must not merely "attain" but "reverse the modern religious current in its depths"; *Œuvres*, vol. 9, p. 161.

99. *Le Christique* (1955). *Le Cœur de la Matière* (1950): Like love itself, Christianity possesses "the astonishing power to transform everything." In the *Christique* he wrote on March 23, 1955: I only hope to have put "a little more to the point some things that I have repeated a hundred times."

100. Letters of October 15, 1916 (*The Making of a Mind*, p. 132), August 15, 1936, etc. All effort at progress among Catholics must be tested and pursued "in the Church by a prayerful and community research": *L'Ame du Monde* (*Ecrits . . .* , p. 231).

101. *The Divine Milieu*, p. 69: "Our faith imposes on us the right and the duty to throw ourselves into the things of the earth," etc. Letter of April 10, 1934, apropos of the death of his friend Dr. Black: "In my distress following Black's death, and in the stifling atmosphere of 'agnostic' condolences that surrounded it, I swore to myself . . . to fight more vigorously than ever to give hope to man's work and inquiry" (*Letters from a Traveller*, p. 202).

102. See, for example, to Léontine Zanta, *Op. cit.*, pp. 52–53.

103. Cf. P. Teilhard and M. Blondel, *Correspondence*, pp. 159–160. In this work, and in our two preceding ones, we have studied at length these essential aspects of Père Teilhard's spirituality.

Part Two

1. *The Vision of the Past*, pp. 51–79.

2. *Œuvres*, vol. 6. Cf. Etienne Borne, "Matière et esprit dans la philosophie de Teilhard de Chardin" in *Recherches et débats*, 40 (1962), p. 50. "Teilhard's procedure . . . deploys itself into one vast proof for the existence of God."

3. We have analyzed this opuscule in *Teilhard de Chardin . . .* , part II: "Note on Teilhard's Apologetics," pp. 129–132.

4. *Quelques réflexions sur la conversion du monde* (1936); cited in *Teilhard de Chardin and the Mystery of Christ*, p. 34.

5. The Exposition of the three proofs will be found in: Msgr. Bruno de Solages, "Les preuves teilhardiennes de Dieu" in the collective work *L'Homme devant Dieu* (collection "Théologie," 1964), vol. 3, pp. 125–132. See below, Ms p. 48.

6. *Letters from a Traveller*, pp. 70–71. Cf. *The Religion . . .* , pp. 182–183.

7. *L'Energie humaine* (1937); *Œuvres*, vol. 6, p. 173.

8. *The Grand Option* (1939) (*The Future of Man*, p. 41), Cf. *Œuvres*, vol. 9, pp. 68 and 110. Cf. *Le Christianisme dans le Monde* (1933): we must eliminate every hypothesis which "would render the universe absurd" (*Œuvres*, vol. 9, p. 136).

9. *L'Energie humaine, loc. cit.*

10. Letter of August 22, 1928 to Léontine Zanta (*Op. cit.*, p. 89.)

11. Paris: Editions universitaires (1961), p. 105. See *Teilhard de Chardin . . .* , pp. 133–136 and p. 188.

12. Cf. *Du Cosmos à la Cosmogenèse* (1951) (*Œuvres*, vol. 7, p. 265). See also *Does Mankind Move Biologically upon Itself?* (*The Future of Man*, pp. 258–259).

13. See especially pages 26 to 31 (4th ed., 1909; Paris: Armand Colin).

14. *The Phenomenon of Man*, p. 151. Cf. *Man's Place in Nature* (New York: Harper & Row, Publishers, 1966), pp. 83–85.

15. *The Phenomenon of Man*, p. 140, note 1: "The 'galaxy' of living forms constitutes . . . a vast 'orthogenetic' movement of involution on an ever-greater complexity and consciousness."

16. *Man's Place in the Universe: Reflections on Complexity* (November, 1942) (*The Vision of the Past*, pp. 222 and 227–228). *La Centrologie* (December 12, 1944); *Œuvres*, vol. 7, pp. 103–104. *Comment je vois* (August 26, 1948), nos. 1–5. *Man's Place in Nature*, p. 23, etc.

17. *L'Atomisme de l'Esprit* (1941) (*Œuvres*, vol. 7, p. 35).

18. A.-D. Sertillanges, O.P., who takes his inspiration from Teilhard in *Dieu ou rien* (Paris: Flammarion, 1933), vol. 1, p. 117: "Intelligence . . . is, in the phenomenon, the supreme achievement of life on earth." Letter to Auguste Valensin, December 31, 1926: "For the last two years above all I have had the impression of being gradually attracted to the study of humanity—not the pre-historic but the present one." Norb. M. Luyten, O.P., "Réflexions sur la méthode de Teilhard de Chardin" in the *Festschrift* presented to Père Bochenski (Fribourg, Switzerland, 1965), p. 294: "In Virtue of his work of paleontology, Teilhard discovers man as the meeting point of this immense evolutionary process. . . . This man is not only the one whose fossil remains he encounters in any particular excavation; he is equally—and even more so—the man living today. For, and this is an unshakable conviction of Teilhard, if we can decipher the fragments which the past has bequeathed us, it is only because of the present that we have under our gaze."

19. *L'Esprit de la Terre* (*Œuvres*, vol. 6, p. 35).

20. *The Phenomenon of Man*, p. 36. "Not simply progress of life but advent of all life," comments Jean Piveteau in speaking about the appearance of man (*Colloque de Vezelay, 1965*).

21. *The Singularities of the Human Species* in *The Appearance of Man* (New York: Harper & Row, Publishers, 1965), pp. 268–269. *Evolution of the Idea of Evolution* (1950): "Initially, that is to say a century ago, man considered himself first of all as a simple observer; then after Darwin, as a simple branch of evolution. But now as a result of this incorporation in biogenesis, he is beginning to perceive that the principal shoot of the tree of earthly Life passes through him. Life does not diversify by chance, in all directions. It shows an absolute direction of progress towards the values of growing consciousness; and on this principal axis man is the most advanced term that we know. . . . He is now in process of recapturing his leadership. No longer stable, but in movement; no longer standing at the center but acting as the leading shoot of the world in growth. Neo-anthropocentrism no longer of position, but of direction in evolution" (*The Vision of the Past*, pp. 246–247).

22. And again: "By means of space, the universe grasps me and swallows me up like a speck; by means of thought I grasp it."

23. *La Peur de l'existence* (1949) (*Œuvres*, vol. 7, pp. 191–195).

24. Etienne Borne, *De Pascal à Teilhard de Chardin* (Clermont-Ferrand, 1962), pp. 36 and 42.

25. Letter of 1935.

26. M. de Gandillac, "Pascal et le silence du monde" in *Blaise Pascal, l'homme et l'œuvre* (Cahiers de Royaumont, Philosophie, I, 1956), pp. 342–385. Cf. Georges Poulet, "Pascal et le sphère admirable" in *Esprit*, 233 (December, 1955), pp. 1833–1849.

27. "L'incroyance moderne, cause profonde et remède" in *La Vie intellectuelle*, October 25, 1923. Cf. Etienne Borne, *op. cit.*, p. 49: "The problem of time would not be as symmetrical as that of space. Although Pascal found in extenstion only an indefinite silence (vainly begun again) in which no situation is qualitatively privileged, in which nothing can be called beginning, center or end, Teilhard de Chardin describes a length of time which develops on a rhythm of growing acceleration toward a last and final end which will then rightly be called 'the Omega point,' " etc. "The last word of Pascal the philosopher was one of interrogation. . . . The last word of Teilhard the philosopher is one of affirmation . . ." (p. 50).

28 *How May We Conceive and Hope* . . . (1950) (*The Future of Man*, p. 285).

29. *L'Union créatrice* (*Ecrits* . . . , pp. 177–178). He even adds—but we are not yet at this point in our journey—that this presupposes a "properly creative" activity. Note of February 18, 1916: "The world is a series of things created one in favor of the other, life in favor of certain dynamic equilibrium—spiritual thought in favor of a certain cerebral

development—grace in favor of a certain moral perfectioning. . . ." Cf. Etienne Borne, *Recherches et débats*, 40, p. 57: "The duality of matter and spirit is in no way suppressed by Teilhard," etc.

30. J.-G. Donders, P.A., *L'Intelligibilité de l'évolution selon A.-D. Sertillanges, O.P.* (thesis of the Gregorian University, 1961), pp. 3 and 21.

31. Letter of May 4, 1931: "He doesn't see that the cosmos holds together not by matter but by spirit" (*Letters from a Traveller*, p. 177), etc.

32. *The Phenomenon of Man*, p. 43. *Du Cosmos à la Cosmogenèse* (1951), on the "Materia matrix" ["*matrix Matter*"]: "the final point of equilibrium of the cosmic movement" comes from the side "of the super-structure or 'ultra-composition,' " that is to say, the spirit. *Œuvres*, vol. 7, pp. 266–267.

33. *Science et Christ* (1920) (*Œuvres*, vol. 9, p. 55. Cf. Piet Smulders, *op. cit.*, pp. 60–67).

34. *Esquisse d'un Univers personnel* (1936) (*Œuvres*, vol. 6, p. 747); cf. Ms p. 56, below. *L'Union créatrice* (1917) (*Ecrits . . .* , pp. 178–179).

35. Thus the third paragraph of *Comment je crois* (1934) is entitled: "La foi en l'immortalité" ["*Faith in Immortality*"]. Cf. *L'Energie humaine* (1937): "The cosmic phenomenon of spiritualization must be irreversible"; *Œuvres*, vol. 6, p. 196. See also *Man's Place in the Universe: Reflections on Complexity* (*The Vision of the Past*, pp. 230–231); *Œuvres*, vol. 9, pp. 125 and 279–280, etc.

36. *The Singularities of the Human Species* (1954) (*The Appearance of Man*, p. 215).

37. *Man's Place in Nature*, p. 114.

38. *La Vie cosmique* (1916) (*Ecrits . . .* , p. 37, etc.). *Note sur le Christ universel* (1920): "the value of souls *in* themselves, that is, the value of the world . . ." (*Œuvres*, vol. 9, p. 42). Cf. *Teilhard de Chardin . . .* , pp. 145–147.

39. *The Phenomenon of Man*, p. 61.

40. *Œuvres*, vol. 7, pp. 302–303. *Man's Place in Nature*, p. 33: "The universe . . . falls from above into continually more advanced forms of arrangement." *The Singularities . . .* (*The Appearance of Man*, p. 215).

41. *Esquisse d'un Univers personnel* (1946) (*Œuvres*, vol. 6, p. 87). One final time the dilemma will be posed, and the duality described, in *Le Christique* (1955): "Entropy or convergence? In other words, is it in the direction of the disordered-unconscious (materialistic solution) or on the contrary of the Ordered-conscious (spiritualistic solution) that the universe ultimately falls on itself in equilibrium?"

42. *La convergence de l'Univers* (*Œuvres*, vol. 7, p. 302). Cf. François Meyer, "L'Evolution se dirige-t-elle vers un terme defini dans le temps?" in *Cahiers Pierre Teilhard de Chardin*, 4 (1963), pp. 90–98.

43. Cf. *Life and the Planets* (1945) (*The Future of Man*, pp. 122–123). *The Phenomenon of Man*, pp. 225–233.

44. *Œuvres*, vol. 7, pp. 151–152 (partly cited: "seen . . . divine" in

P. Teilhard and M. Blondel, *Correspondence*, p. 149). *Super-Humanité*
. . . (1943); vol. 9, p. 208. *Man's Place in Nature*, p. 108.

45. *Aldo Locatelli, Dio e miracolo conoscibile al di la della scienza* (Ed.
La scuola cattolica, 1963), p. 121.

46. We have explained ourselves in *The Religion* . . . , especially chapter 9: *"The Legitimacy of Teilhard's Extrapolation,"* pp. 206–220.

47. *Réflexions sur la probabilité scientifique et les conséquences religieuses d'un Ultra-humain* (1951) (*Œuvres*, vol. 7, pp. 279–291).

48. Pages 115–116.

49. We have sketched a critical examination in chapter 16 of *The Religion* . . . : *"Faith and Intelligibility,"* pp. 173–184.

50. Msgr. de Solages, *loc. cit.* (Part II, footnote 5). The author treats
the subject more in depth in a work to appear shortly.

51. *De la science à la foi, Teilhard de Chardin* (1965), pp. 150–153:
(a) Exigencies of a realized convergence; (b) in the more precise perspective of thought; (c) in the more precise perspective of love.

52. Père Valverde of the University of Comillas (Spain) presented a
report to the international Thomistic Congress of Rome (September
1965) on *Evolucionismo Teilhardiano y quinta Via* (*Proceedings* . . . ,
vol. 1, pp. 295–301). In another report of this same congress, Père
Marcel Duquesne of the Catholic Faculty of Lille made an analogous
comparison ("The proof for God through the governance of things").

53. *Œuvres*, vol. 9, p. 226.

54. Claude Cuénot, *Pierre Teilhard de Chardin* (1958), pp. 336–337.

55. *Man's Place in Nature*, p. 121. Cf. *Comment je vois* (1948), no. 13.

56. *Comment je vois*, no. 20. *L'Union créatrice* in *Ecrits* . . . , pp. 181–
184.

57. Piet Smulders, *op. cit.*, pp. 278–279: "In this respect, the movement
of the Teilhardian thought does not differ essentially from forms of a
classical apologetics."

58. *The Phenomenon of Man*, p. 269. *The Mass on the World* (1923):
"The world travails, not to bring forth within itself some supreme reality,
but to find its consummation through a union with a pre-existing Being"
(*Hymn of the Universe*, p. 31).

59. *Action et Activation* (August 9, 1945) (*Œuvres*, vol. 9, p. 226). *La
Vie cosmique* (*Ecrits* . . . , pp. 5 and 183). *L'Union créatrice*, etc.

60. *Comment je crois* (1934). *Sommaire de ma perspective phénoméno-
logique du Monde* (1954), p. 2, etc. "The 'Conic' Transposition of
Action" (*The New Spirit*) (1942): "ultra-conscious, ultra-personalized,
ultra-present" in *The Future of Man*, p. 92.

61. *L'Energie humaine* (1937) (*Œuvres*, vol. 6, p. 180).

62. *The Human Rebound of Evolution and Its Consequences* (1947)
(*The Future of Man*, p. 207).

63. *Esquisse d'un Univers personnel* (1936) (*Œuvres*, vol. 6, p. 89).

64. *Le Phenomène spirituel* (1936) (*Œuvres,* vol. 6, p. 136; cited in *Teilhard de Chardin . . . ,* p. 24).

65. *Esquisse d'un Univers personnel* (1936) (*Œuvres,* vol. 6, p. 103). *Du Cosmos à la Cosmogenèse* (March 15, 1951), *Œuvres,* vol. 7, p. 271, etc.

66. *The Phenomenon of Man,* p. 270; "central focus, necessarily autonomous" (p. 262), note. *Man's Place in the Universe: Reflections on Complexity* (1942): "Place [focus] of irreversibility" (*The Vision of the Past,* p. 231. On the simplicity and "complexity" of the Existence of God: *Esquisse d'un Univers personnel, Œuvres,* vol. 6, pp. 75 and 86.

67. See also *La Centrologie,* no. 24 (*Œuvres,* vol. 7, p. 119).

68. *The Divine Milieu,* p. 139.

69. *La Centrologie,* no. 24 (*Œuvres,* vol. 7, p. 119).

70. *Comment je vois,* no. 20. *Réflexions sur le bonheur* (*Cahiers . . . ,* vol. 2, p. 63).

71. *The Phenomenon of Man,* pp. 268–270. *The Singularities of the Human Species,* appendix (March 24, 1954) (*The Appearance of Man,* pp. 272–273. Père Teilhard, we perceive, was not tempted to imitate the action which ambitiously envisages surmounting the ultimate value of love and transcending the transcendence of the personal God," an action which in reality "lets itself docilely be carried away by a pre-Christian and pre-personal spiritual current": Jacques-Albert Cuttat, introduction to R.-C. Zaehner, *Inde, Israël, Islam,* tr. Eva Meyerovitch, 1965, p. 17.

72. Remember that in Père Teilhard's language unification and identification are opposed. The first is also differentiation, personalization. Supremely unifying, God is "supremely personalizing": *Comment je vois,* no. 20, etc.

73. *Esquisse d'une dialectique de l'esprit* (1946) (*Œuvres,* vol. 7, pp. 154–156). *Comment je crois* (1934): "And since in that way a superior sphere of the Personal and personal relations now stands out for me, I am beginning to suspect that attractions and directions of an intellectual nature might well surround me and speak to me."

74. *Teilhard de Chardin et la pensée catholique. Colloque de Venise* (Paris, 1965), pp. 88–89.

75. Letter of May 25, 1923 (cited in *The Religion . . . ,* p. 202).

76. *Comment je vois,* no. 22.

77. See the terms cited in P. Teilhard and M. Blondel, *Correspondence,* the chapter entitled: " 'Ascent' and 'Descent' in the Work of Teilhard de Chardin" (pp. 143–160). Teilhard, nicely states Georges Crespy (*op. cit.,* p. 107), "does not dissimulate the 'passage to another genre' which constitutes the act of faith."

78. *Mon Univers* of 1924 (*Œuvres,* vol. 9, p. 81). We can here apply what Père Henri Bouillard says concerning Blondel, in *Blondel et le Christianisme* (1961), p. 162: "To establish that the mystery of the Mediator resolves the philosophic dilemma is not to require the Incarna-

tion, but rather to profit from the light brought to bear by the notion of the Incarnation which has been discovered through other means."

79. *Mon Univers* of 1924 (*Œuvres*, vol. 9, p. 84 (cited in *The Religion . . .* , p. 322, note 48).

80. *Social Heredity and Progress* (1938) (*The Future of Man*, p. 34). Such is the "Christian humanist's" vision of things.

81. Note of October 17, 1918. *L'Union créatrice* (November, 1917): "Christ is not, of course, the center that all things here below could by their natural powers aspire to wed. Destination to Christ is an unexpected and gratuitous gift and grace of the Creator. But it is still true that, etc." (*Ecrits . . .* , p. 195; cited in *The Design of Teilhard de Chardin*, p. 281, note 34). Reasoning to the interior of our world, Père Teilhard therefore no longer habitually envisaged the hypothesis of any "intermediary whatever" or a "vague focus of convergence." He had done so at least once, in *L'Ame du Monde* (1918). See the note which precedes this text in *Ecrits . . .* , pp. 217–219. Teilhard's thought on this point is in part an echo of Pierre Rousselot's thought, as expounded in the unpublished study "Idéalisme et Thomisme," written in 1908 and revised in 1911.

82. *Mon Univers* of 1924 (*Œuvres*, vol. 9, p. 82, January 29, 1918): "By his gospel of renunciation Christ has established a new Omega in the Cosmos, but it is for us ("Vos estis sine intelligentia?" ["Are you also without understanding?"]) to bridge the gap between this Omega and the natural becoming of the Cosmos." Cf. *The Phenomenon of Man*, p. 298, note.

83. *Ma position intellectuable* (New York, April, 1948).

84. *La Mystique de la Science* (1939) (*Œuvres*, vol. 6, pp. 220–221).

85. *Ma position intellectuelle* (April, 1948); text published in *Les Etudes philosophiques* in 1955 under the title *La Pensée du Père Teilhard de Chardin par lui-même*, p. 580.

86. *What Should We Think of Transformism?* (1930) (*The Vision of the Past*, p. 157).

87. Response to an inquiry of the periodical *Esprit, Catholicisme et Science* (1946) (*Œuvres*, vol. 9, pp. 238–240). Cf. *Réflexions sur deux formes d'esprit* (1950) (*Œuvres*, vol. 7, p. 236).

88. *La Vie Cosmique* (1916); *Ecrits . . .* , p. 9.

89. *La Centrologie* (December 13, 1944), introduction (*Œuvres*, vol. 7, pp. 105–106). *Man's Place in the Universe: Reflections on Complexity* (November 15, 1942) (*The Vision of the Past*, p. 217). *L'Union créatrice* (*Ecrits . . .* , p. 180), and other analogous texts.

90. Letter of February 25, 1929.

91. Letter of November 20, 1918 (*The Making of a Mind*, p. 256). *La Peur de l'existence* (January 26, 1949) (*Œuvres*, vol. 7, p. 196; cited in *Teilhard de Chardin . . .* , p. 144, note 6).

92. We have broached the subject on several occasions in *The Religion . . .* , and especially in chapter 15 ("A Reversal of Method"), pp. 161–

172; also in P. Teilhard and M. Blondel, *Correspondence*, pp. 123–135: "The Aims and Scope of the Work of Teilhard de Chardin."

93. *Teilhard de Chardin et la pensée catholique, Colloque de Venise,* p. 19.

94. *Réflexions sur la methode de Teilhard de Chardin,* in the volume of *Festschrift* presented to Père Bochenski (Fribourg, Switzerland, 1965), pp. 295 and 317.

95. *De la science à la foi,* p. 9.

96. *Colloque de Venise,* p. 33. One would willingly apply to Teilhard a judgment analogous to that passed by Père Sertillanges on Claude Bernard: "He builds a bridge between physiology and metaphysics"; *La philosophie de Claude Bernard* (1964), p. 7.

97. *The Human Rebound of Evolution and Its Consequences* (September 23, 1947) (*The Future of Man,* p. 210).

98. On a few other aspects of this optimism: Jean Bastaire, "Teilhard l'impatiante," *Cahiers universitaeres catholiques* (December, 1965–January, 1966), pp. 146–159.

99. Cf. *Teilhard de Chardin . . . ,* part II, ch. 4: "Faith and Analogy," pp. 161–168.

100. *Comment je crois.*

101. He wrote to Père Auguste Valensin, May 27, 1923: "No matter what the cost; it is necessary to cling to faith *in a meaning,* and *in a term,* of (even natural) human agitation, since without this faith, nothing more can come to legitimate the law of our action before our reason. But at first sight appearances are contrary, and the chaos and divergence appear to dominate the history of life."

102. *L'Energie humaine* (1937) (*Œuvres,* vol. 6, pp. 173–174).

103. Cf. *La lutte contre la multitude* (*Ecrits . . . ,* pp. 120–122).

104. *Réflexions sur le bonheur* (Peking, December 28, 1943) (*Cahiers Pierre Teilhard de Chardin,* 2, pp. 55–58).

105. *Esquisse d'un Univers personnel* (1936) (*Œuvres,* vol. 6, p. 105: "There is nothing more beatifying than the union attained: but nothing more laborious than the purtsuit of the union").

106. *The Singularities of the Human Species* (*The Appearance of Man,* p. 106. *The Making of a Mind,* p. 214. *La Parole attendue* (1940) (*Cahiers . . . ,* 4, p. 28). *La Vie cosmique* (*Ecrits . . . ,* pp. 54–57). Preface to Marguerite Teilhard de Chardin, *L'energie spirituelle de la souffrance* (1951), pp. 9–11. *Mon univers* of 1924 (*Œuvres,* vol. 9, pp. 88–92 and 97–102, etc.). He was well aware that Christian charity is not natural to man—and he was even reproached in very inconsiderate fashion for having realistically established this. *Fiunt, non nascuntur Christiani* [*Christians are made not born*].

107. *Esquisse d'un Univers personnel* (*Œuvres,* vol. 6, p. 89; cited—from the words, "to preserve" on—in *Teilhard de Chardin . . . ,* p. 178).

108. *Comment je crois* (1934).

109. See, for example, *Le Coeur de la Matière* (1950), p. 32. Already *La Grande Monade* (1918) (*Ecrits . . .*, pp. 237–248). *The Divine Milieu*, p. 137: "That I may not succumb to the temptation to curse the universe and him who made it. . . ." Cf. *Teilhard de Chardin . . .*, pp. 121–123. M. Barthélemy-Madaule, *Bergson et Teilhard de Chardin* (1962), pp. 411–421. Claude Cuénot, "L'angoisse contemporaine, un essai de réponse," in *Cahiers de vie franciscaine*, 33 (1962).

110. *The End of the Species* (December 9) (*The Future of Man*, p. 303). Cf. *Le goût de vivre* (November, 1950) (*Œuvres*, vol. 7, pp. 239–251). *Some Reflections* on the *Spiritual Repercussions of the Atom Bomb* (1946) (*The Future of Man*, pp. 145–146).

111. *La Peur de l'existence* (1949) (*Œuvres*, vol. 7, p. 197).

112. *Réflexions sur le bonheur* (1943) (*Cahiers . . .*, 2, p. 60).

113. Cf. Pierre Rousselot, S.J., *Etudes* of September 5, 1911: "Who will cause our contemporaries to experience this zest for life, this profound and ineffable love for existence, this fervent optimism, this grave, profound, almost infinite tenderness for humanity, which rises from every page of the Angelic Doctor?"

114. Cf. Etienne Borne, *De Pascal à Teilhard de Chardin* (Clermont-Ferrand, 1962), pp. 67–68: "Despite dubious polemics which obscure our view, it is in the Thomist tradition—many of whose characteristics are nevertheless allergic to Teilhard de Chardin—that the Teilhardian thought is situated: rehabilitation of a nature in itself veracious and good, rational description of man and of the world according to concepts drawn from an experimental and positive science, proof for the existence of the absolute through the very movement of things which designates a prime mover or an Omega point: all these traits are common to St. Thomas Aquinas and Teilhard de Chardin." See also M. M. Labourdette, O.P., *Le péché originel et les origines de l'homme* (1953), pp. 127 and 145–146. Olivier-A. Rabut, O.P., *Teilhard de Chardin* (New York: Sheed and Ward, 1961), p. 166. Claude Cuénot, "Situation de Teilhard de Chardin" (*Bulletin de la Société industrielle de Mulhouse*, 1963, no. 712, p. 25; and, citing E. Borne, p. 26). P. Teilhard and M. Blondel *Correspondence*, pp. 111 and 114–115, etc.

115. Letter to Léontine Zanta, January 26, 1936 (*Op. cit.*, pp. 127–128), etc. Cf. March 16, 1919: "That which nourishes my entire interior life is the *relish* for *Being*, satisfied in God, our Lord"; "May our Lord preserve in me the relish for Being and the vision that Being is Himself!" See *Teilhard de Chardin . . .*, p. 84.

116. He wrote on February 25, 1920: "It seems to me that I brought a certain "Physics of the Spirit" nearly up to date. . . . It is a kind of reduction of the universe to the spiritual on the physical (not metaphysical) plane, which for me has the happy corollary of legitimizing the preservation of persons (that is, the "immortality" of souls) in the universe."

117. *L'activation de l'Energie humain* (1953) (*Œuvres*, vol. 7, p. 413).

Notes

118. Joseph Perini, C.M. *Utrum argumentando ex desiderio naturali immortalitatis, S. Thomas apodictice evincat animam humanam esse immortalem;* in *Divus Thomas* (Piacenza, 1965), p. 383: "It is most certainly a question of an apodictic proof, which namely is able of itself to impart perfect certitude to the intellect." Cf. *The Religion . . .* , pp. 174–179.

119. *The Phenomenon of Man*, pp. 231–233.

120. Letter of April 10, 1934 (*Letters from a Traveller*, p. 202, etc. Cf. *Lettres à Léontine Zanta*, pp. 134–135).

121. *Le goût de vivre* (1950) (*Œuvres*, vol. 7, p. 246).

122. *Le Christique* (1955) (cited in *Teilhard de Chardin . . .* , p. 149, note 30).

123. *Hominization* (*The Vision of the Past*, pp. 72 and 75–76). *Man's Place in Nature*, pp. 91–92, 107–108, etc.

124. *Place de la technique dans une biologie générale de l'humanité* (1947) (*Œuvres*, vol. 7, p. 168; cited in *Teilhard de Chardin . . .* , p. 99).

125. Page 120. Cf. *La Vie cosmique* (*Ecrits . . .* , p. 56): "All energy is equally powerful for good or evil." *Mon Univers* of 1924 (*Œuvres*, vol. 9, pp. 112–113). See *Teilhard de Chardin . . .* , part I, ch. 13, pp. 97–108. It is in this sense that Teilhard would have agreed to say with M. Albert Vandel (L'évolutionisme du Père Teilhard de Chardin," in *Les Etudes philosophiques*, 1965, p. 463): "Man can achieve all things but also fail." Likewise, by saying that "it would be easier . . . to prevent the earth from revolving than to prevent mankind from becoming totalized," or again that "the human social group cannot escape from certain irreversible laws of evolution," Teilhard certainly intends to say nothing which would be "a humiliating threat to our liberty": *The Directions and Conditions of the Future* (1948) (*The Future of Man*, pp. 229–232). Anti-Teilhardian prejudice does not prevent an intelligent man from writing: "The conception of an assured and irreversible noogenesis could certainly be only a manifestation of the eternal quietism to which Pelagianism fatally leads" (André Thérive in *Ecrits de Paris*, February, 1964, p. 102).

126. See *The Religion . . .* , ch. 10: "Evolution and Freedom," pp. 108–120; P. Teilhard and M. Blondel, *Correspondence*, pp. 106–108 and p. 159. Cf. *A Note on Progress* (1920) (*The Future of Man*, p. 19), etc. "Born with intelligence, the temptation to revolt must constantly vary and grow up with it" (Cl. Cuénot, "Situation . . . ," *loc. cit.*, p. 11).

127. *Some Reflections on the Spiritual Repercussions of the Atom Bomb* (*The Future of Man*, pp. 147–148).

128. Georges Crespy, *De la science à la théologie, essai sur Teilhard de Chardin* (Cahiers théologiques, 54; ed. Delachaux et Niestle, Neuchâtel, Switzerland, 1965), p. 105.

129. *The Phenomenon of Man*, pp. 115 and 148. *Bulletin de la Société*

géologique de France, 1946, p. 501, etc. P. Teilhard and M. Blondel, *Correspondence,* pp. 108–109.

130. See also *La vie cosmique* (*Ecrits . . .* , pp. 25–28): "The segregation of humanity."

131. This is the doctrine of the Fathers of the Church. Thus St. Hilary of Poitiers: "But he, containing the nature of the universe in himself through the assumption of flesh"; "He asssumed in himself the nature of all flesh"; "he assumed the body of all of us" (Migne, PL, 10, 409; 9., 1025; CSEL, 22, 108), etc. Origen, *In Psalmum* 36, hom. 2, no. 1: "For Christ, whose body is the genus of every man, and indeed perhaps of every creature of the universe" (Migne, P. 6, 12, 1330). Cf. St. Cyril of Alexandria *Against Nestorius* 1. I, C.1 (Migne, P. G., 76, 17). St. Thomas, *Summa,* part three, question 8, art. 3: "By being accepted generally according to the whole time of the world, Christ is the head of all men, but according to various grades . . ."

132. Letter of October 9, 1916 (*The Making of a Mind,* p. 130). *Le Prêtre* (1918): "You have made known to me the essential vocation of the world to be achieved through a part chosen with all its being in the fullness of your Word incarnate" (*Ecrits . . .* , p. 286).

133. Notes of February 8 and July 19, 1916; April 9 and November 16, 1918.

134. *Les Noms de la Matière* (1919) (*Ecrits . . .* , p. 429). Letter of January 9, 1917: "For me the real earth is that chosen part of the universe, still almost universally dispensed and in the course of gradual segregation, but which is little by little taking on body and form in Christ" (*The Making of a Mind,* p. 165).

135. It is found in *The Divine Milieu:* "The whole process out of which the New Earth is gradually born is an *aggregation* underlaid by a segregation" (p. 147); "Segregation and aggregation. Separation of the evil elements of the world, and 'co-adunation' of the elemental worlds that each faithful spirit constructs around him in work and pain, etc." (p. 150).

136. Although Paul also says: "All Israel should be saved" (Rom. 11, 26), he does not pretend to decide the fate of each individual. Cf. St. Augustine, *In Joannem,* tract 6, no. 26, apropos of schisms with a reference to Canticles 6, 9: "Why have you destroyed my dove? No, you have not destroyed her; you have destroyed your own insides; for while you have been destroyed, the dove has remained intact." See our book, *Catholicism* (New York: Sheed & Ward, Inc.; Mentor-Omega edition, 1964), ch. 8, pp. 134–150.

137. Etienne Borne, in *Recherches et débats,* 40 (1962), p. 64.

138. Helmut de Terra, *Memories of Teilhard de Chardin,* tr. J. Maxwell Brownjohn (New York and Evanston: Harper & Row, Publishers, 1964), p. 121.

139. Père Norbert M. Luyten has judiciously observed in this respect that "out of fear of an overly naive—or excessively difficult—cosmology our thought has become in great part a-cosmic and remains prisoner

of an auto-reflection that is a little insipid. Teilhard, he concludes, has at least the merit of indicating "the immense and urgent task facing us." *Teilhard de Chardin, Nouvelles perspectives du savoir?* (Fribourg, Switzerland, 1965), pp. 66–67.